THE BEST-SELL
BECOMING THE

DATE YOURSELF WELL

The Ultimate Engagement Plan

DR. SHANNON GULBRANSON

Published by Insight International, Inc.
contact@freshword.com
www.freshword.com
918-493-1718

The author is not a medical doctor, nor does she dispense medical advice or prescribe the use of any technique as a form of treatment for physical, emotional, psychological, or medical problems without the advice of a physician, either directly or indirectly. The intent of the author is only to offer information of a general nature to help you in your search for emotional and spiritual wellbeing and engagement. The author has successfully used the *Date Yourself Well* Engagements with many clients, however does not guarantee specific results. In the event you use any of the information in this book for yourself, the author and the publisher assume no responsibility for your actions.

Cover Design: Pablo Aguilar, www.webdesigncreator.com
Editing: Michelle Mason, Anni Caylor, Glenyce Gulbranson

ISBN: 978-1-943361-37-3
E-Book ISBN: 978-1-943361-10-6

Printed in the United States of America.

PRAISE FOR *DATE YOURSELF WELL*

"Lennon was right! If enduring love is what you're after, *Date Yourself Well* will guide you on a transformative journey to the happily ever after you seek. Dr. Shannon's thoughtful, empowering, and inspirational treatise will hold a treasured spot on your bedside nightstand."

— Evan Michael Zislis,
Author of *Aphrodisiac: Clearing the Cluttered Path to Epic Love, Great Sex & Relationships that Last*
and the Amazon International Best-seller,
ClutterFree Revolution: Simplify Your Stuff, Organize Your Life & Save the World

"As an acknowledged Relationship Expert and author, I tend to be critical in my praise. I have been fortunate to be with Dr. Shannon personally, and within a group dynamic as a participant. She is unique in her perspective as it relates to women, men, relationships, and love. Astute and powerful as a leader, her clarity and experience in causing breakthrough results is a gift worth reading. *Date Yourself Well* is unquestionably a worthwhile read for anyone committed to deeply understanding his or her heart, the keys to experiencing true love, and living a great love...life."

— Martin Cohen, Relationship Expert and
Best-selling Author of *Gender Balancing: An Evolutionary Model for Elevating Relationships from Mediocre to EXTRAORDINARY*

"Dr. Shannon's fresh new perspective on dating yourself well, and fully engaging in life, is powerfully relevant and highly needed in today's modern era. Through a proven, effective twelve-week process (complete with Weekly Dates), *Date Yourself Well* takes the reader through the course of a new type of engagement. A full engagement with herself, and the life she lives."

— John Mason, Best-Selling Author of
An Enemy Called Average

"*Date Yourself Well* is a reminder that before you go out searching for love, make sure you have found it inside yourself first. Love and nurture yourself and be your best companion."

— Melanie Young, Author of *Fearless Fabulous! Lessons on Living Life on Your Terms* and *Getting Things Off My Chest*

"Through the sorrows and perils of the stereotypical NYC dating scene, I was no exception to this cliché experience. Years of picking a partner based on what society told me was correct (or maybe instant gratification) led me to believe who I was with *could be* "Mr. Right", yet it always ended in heartache. What I realized through multiple life coaching sessions with Dr. Shannon, using her *Date Yourself Well* program, was that the real heartache I was feeling was disappointment with myself. I knew deep down what my heart and soul needed, but didn't follow that voice. Dr. Shannon's words gave me self-clarity, and taught me to love myself with the same intention I wished to be loved and love another. The most rewarding experience was taking myself to a beach with a bottle of wine, halfway around the world, and being happier than I could last remember…loving ME, and enjoying time with ME. Thank you, Dr. Shannon, for awakening my inner love and voice! You are a blessing."

— Heather Emerson,
Founder of Resume Your Success

"*Date Yourself Well* is truly inspiring! Wow! Anyone can open it, and find what they are seeking at the time. It's a book that needs to be at our nightstand when we may have those *Less Than Optimal* (L.T.O.) days, and need to get back on track. Reading it and being coached by Dr. Shannon has been so good for me. It was the key that unlocked my heart so the healing could begin. The transformation doesn't just happen without showing up and doing the work. So I invite my *Bestie* to stand up and be recognized. Then I go to my *Heart House* for love. Learning to love ourselves first, in order to share with others, is a challenge. We are told throughout life to be selfless and put others first. It is a fine line. But when we get it, we got it. I'm so thankful to be a part of your world!"

— Mary Schumacher,
Happy *Date Yourself Well* Coaching Client

DEDICATION

I dedicate this book to my precious and loving parents, Marvin and Glenyce Gulbranson. They've always been my biggest supporters and greatest examples of true, unconditional, lifelong love. A couple months before I released the *e-book* version of *Date Yourself Well*, we celebrated the changing of my name back to the one my Daddy and Mommy gave me on the day I was born: Shannon Gulbranson. ☺ *(They were so honored.)*

Three days after we launched, the e-book became a bestseller. *(I'm so grateful. I was very happy, and immediately called them to share the good news.)* Two days later, both my parents were killed in a car accident. After almost fifty-four years of marriage, they entered eternal life…in love and together.

My last conversations with each of them were about the book. They were so excited. They told me how proud they were, and how much they loved me. I told them the same, and thanked them for always believing in, and loving me so well.

It's in their loving memory that I share the powerful message contained within these pages with you today.

Mom and Dad, I love and miss you more than words can say! I wouldn't be who, or where, I am today without you. Thank you for always being there for me with your unconditional love and presence…even now in your absence. XOXO

A NOTE TO YOU, MY DEAR READER

HOW'S YOUR LOVE...LIFE?

If you are holding back in any area of your life, due to "waiting" for the future or feeling "stuck" in the present, this book is for you. It's time to *have,* and no longer *to hold.* Holding on to the past, or living in an "ideal" future, is divorcing you from the present life you would love to passionately live.

Become the great lover of your life.

In today's modern era, the way we view relationships, marriage and family is very different from decades past. Our culture has definitely changed, but what hasn't changed are people. No matter how much our culture has transcended, *we are,* and will remain, humans! And the human experience on planet earth is one that yearns for meaningful relationship and a deeper connectedness.

Social media provides overwhelming evidence of our insatiable desire to share *who* we are with someone. Anyone who will notice and pay attention.

Although at times controversial, we have attempted to define people, preferences, orientation, gender, relationships, and commitment as they relate one to the other. We have defined God as religion instead of Love. We have made attempts at unity and inclusion, while creating division and exclusion. This includes the relationship with love, each other, and ourselves. And yet we have somehow missed defining the relationship that we have with and within ourselves (head + heart, heart and soul). This is not only an issue (and an opportunity) for women, but for all humankind.

In this book, however, I am going to speak directly to women. Yes, *you!* I am writing to ALL women, whether single or not.

If you have never had a *significant other*, or are single due to a breakup, divorce, or death of a loved one, this message is for you. From my own experience, this *new engagement* is long overdue, and must be shared with as many women (young and not so young) as possible.

If you are in a relationship (dating or married), there is vital information here for you too. In fact, I believe this message has the power to prevent broken relationships and divorce. Yes, that's definitely a bold statement, but please keep reading.

These truths have completely transformed my life. As I'm writing to you today, I am living the life of my dreams as a happy, healthy woman. After three divorces over more than a decade of suffering from a disengaged (divorced) heart, I finally learned to date myself well. This led to pursing my dream of living in the Big Apple. I sold or gave away my possessions, except only those that I absolutely loved (and still do, by the way), and followed my heart. No longer suffering from the heaviness of a divorced heart, nor the weight of excess baggage, I arrived in my new city and continue to fall in love with my *simply lovely* life more and more each day. It's been the adventure of a lifetime—one of healing—and a love affair that repeatedly takes my breath away, while increasing my inspiration. I'm fully engaged in the wild romance of successfully dating myself well, building loving relationships, creating the life I love, and prosperously sharing my message with the world. I now live between Minneapolis (home) and New York City (or as I like to call it, "MYCity"), and am continually amazed by the healing power and prosperity of LOVE.

My desire is the same for you. Not that you would necessarily do exactly what I have done, but that you will do what YOU desire. With no more holding back. Follow your heart, my dear.

There is nothing more engaging than waking up every day knowing that I am a great lover of my life.

I am not a medical doctor, licensed counselor, psychologist, psychiatrist, or mental health professional. I am, however, a woman that has lived the devastating consequences of a disengaged heart. Losing *almost* everything, including who I was. *That was then (years ago)*. Speaking from a heart that is healed, and a head + heart that have become one, I am on a mission to teach you everything I've learned about how to live a fully engaged, certain, abundant, moving, purposeful, life of love. *This is now.*

I will show you how. Had I learned to date myself well while I was young, it would have saved me years of heartache, pain, and unnecessary suffering. There's no doubt in my mind that it would have prevented the substantial loss of time, health, and money that my divorce(s) caused.

No matter where you are along your path in life, I have one question to ask you. This question changed my life, and it can change yours too.

When was the last time you were fully engaged in your life?

If your answer is anything other than, "Now," don't worry. It can be.

You can be!

It all starts with a date...a date with you. Today.

For these reasons and more, I thank you in advance for fully engaging in the process of dating yourself well, and for helping me share these revolutionary truths with brave hearts + heads that are ready for a *new kind of dating relationship.* Together we can engage *their* world, and continue to transform *the world.*

xo
Dr. Shannon

CONTENTS

PREFACE

MY PROMISE TO YOU

You will become fully engaged, and fall in love with you in less than ninety days, while discovering a relationship that you never knew existed—not even in fairytales.

I will teach you how to be in a fully engaged, satisfying, healthy relationship with YOU. I will show you how you can go from living a life of *want* to an experience of *desire*. I will help you fall in love with you, and guide you through the proven, effective engagements of *dating yourself well.*

Imagine: No more wondering why you're single. No more longing for "the one." No more waiting to be asked out. No more lonely Friday nights or weekends. No more waiting for the phone call that doesn't come. No more fear of heartache. No more longing for something *more* while in a relationship. No more confusion, disconnection, or despair. No more holding back. No more worry. No more questioning if you're good enough, attractive enough, or lovable enough. No more game playing. No more neediness. No more loss. No more looking for love in all the wrong places. No more blaming. No more excuses. No more suffering. No more bad dates.

Now imagine this: MORE of what you deeply desire. MORE of the love and life you seek. MORE!

You will learn the profound principles of fully engaging in a life you love. One that will keep you IN LOVE, as well as keep you from FALLING OUT OF LOVE...a love that goes beyond "until death do you part."

...AND "THE YOU" SHALL
FINALLY BECOME ONE!

THE PURPOSE

This *new dating relationship* has brought purpose, clarity, adventure, romance, and direction to women who have a desire for more. It has been the guiding force that has led single and married women to explore, and discover the longing that's within them, and the joy of seeing their dreams come true. It has taken women through the gut-wrenching pain of divorce, and into a life of total abundance and blessing. These essential steps have empowered women to become fully expressed, and to live an engaging life of love from the inside, out.

More women today are putting off getting married or having children (or possibly not at all). Instead they are pursuing their dreams of education, becoming entrepreneurs, or traveling the world on a great adventure of discovery. They are consciously and actively choosing this path rather than seeing it as a default to *not* being married.

On the contrary, there are still many women falling in love, getting married, and continuing to pursue their dreams, goals, and desires *while* raising a family. They're also doing it with the ease that comes from being fully engaged in their lives.

However, this is not the case for the majority of women.

Far too many single women continue to make plans for their lives based on the elusive "Mr. Right" whom they hope will eventually sweep in, and rescue them from their dismal days of being single. Or worse yet, they are putting their lives on hold as they wait for some handsome prince to *put a ring on it.*

I know women personally who have not pursued their dreams because they didn't know how it would fit into the stereotypical role of girlfriend, fiancée, wife, and/or mother. I have spoken with young women who are limiting themselves in education or career choices because they think that eventually they won't need it or they won't be able to use it. They fail to ask themselves, "What are my desires? What are my dreams? What am I good at? What is it that I would love to do?

Many married women are discovering the life-altering experience of an unexpected divorce. Or they're living in the overwhelming devastation of feeling lonely and unfulfilled, while desperately longing for something more because they have stopped living a creative, fully engaged life.

Why is it that oftentimes we, as women, don't allow ourselves to think big, and I mean, REALLY BIG, when we think about our opportunities and our future?

It's not too late to start. No matter where you are in your life's journey, it is never too late to start dreaming and creating again. You can sing and follow the song of your soul starting right now.

How many women (and men, for that matter) are not living their dreams, but instead are living their life by default because they took the path that her/his upbringing, family, beliefs, or culture said they "should"? Often denying the quiet voice inside that says *pursue your dreams, and when you are full and fulfilled, you will recognize others in your life who are also whole, healthy, and happy.*

I have always pursued my dreams, but many times I have slowed down, held back, or put myself in a holding pattern because of a relationship, the loss of one, or my idea of what a relationship "should" be.

Please don't get me wrong; I am certainly not saying that true love with another, a lasting relationship, a marriage, and family are not incredibly awesome, and something that many of us desire. I LOVE *LOVE*! I love being in a happy relationship, and I love family. Especially being a mom.

What I'm saying is when you put your entire focus on these things, you can miss something that's absolutely magical, and that *something* could perhaps be the piece (peace) that seems to be missing in your life. It's the most delightful piece of the one-of-a-kind masterpiece that is authentically you.

That missing piece is *YOUR* LOVE. The love you have for you. Not only loving you, but recognizing your divine nature and realizing that this love IS YOU!

Is it possible? It's happened not only for me personally, but for the many incredible clients I've worked with over the years.

After coaching a highly successful physician, she not only fully engaged in her life, but she received a promotion at work, and an increase in salary. She also attracted the man of her dreams. When I asked her what was different, she replied, "I finally love me."

When we began working together, she did it with the heartfelt intention of taking care of herself and her heart. She didn't do so to find a partner, to fix herself, or to attempt to complete herself by finding a man. Instead she had made the decision to find, and love, herself like never before. Unconditionally. Years later she is still living and loving her life, and the love of her life.

One of my happily married clients has an awesome husband. Learning the principles of dating herself well allowed her to finally see firsthand how loving and caring for herself would benefit and strengthen her relationship with him, as well as with others. Her marriage has grown to a whole new level.

Another young, savvy, single New Yorker that I coached, followed her dreams, and did exactly what she said was *impossible* when we first met. She left her day job and began an adventure that took her around the world, while beginning the first steps of launching her own business. She went from feeling trapped and unhappy to living in a state of bliss and freedom; following her heart, traveling the world, and launching a new company.

Personally, I've coached many powerful individuals (women and men) to become fully engaged in living life at a high level of joy, excellence, and abundance.

What once seemed heavy and impossible became light, *ease-y,* and completely possible when she/he found the love (and success) they were searching for within their hearts.

> I will never forget the day
> I woke up to the revelation
> that I was finally living my dream.

It was that day which inspired me to help others, like myself, to not only acknowledge their dreams, but also to *fully engage* with them.

This is my reality now, but it wasn't always this way for me.

I have been happily single, and I have been happily married. I have also been unhappily married, and unhappily single. And I can wholeheartedly tell you this, *HAPPILY* IS BETTER!!!!!! (Can I add some more exclamation points, please?)

The truth is that it's possible for ALL women (and men), regardless of marital or "*non-marital*" status. What matters more than the S, M, D, or P that you pencil in on a document, is the person writing it. YOU HAVE THE POWER AND POSSIBILITY WITHIN YOU!

Whether you are single or not single, can you imagine being able to share and express your voice, desires, and gifts during your lifetime, and have a blast doing it? (Oh, and can I mention also the *possibility* of making a lot of money?)

Yes, it's possible.

If you are courageous enough to follow the steps I've outlined in this book and lead others to do the same, the possibilities are endless. Engage in the process.

Now, I know what you may be thinking, "But I could never do that."

I understand. This is why...

THE PROBLEM

CHAPTER 1

THE *CINDERELLA* SYNDROME

What do you do when "simply meant to be" is not that simple?

Yes, I would like to think that every woman is living her fairytale dream. Unfortunately most women *think* they need to be dating or married to see their dreams come true, or be happy, fulfilled, secure, or complete.

And then on the flip side, the only women that think being single would be a dream come true are the ones who are unhappily married! Trust me, you don't want to be one of them. It's not fun.

What if *happily ever after* doesn't come? What if Prince Charming turns out to be Prince *Not So* Charming or Prince Harming? What if you aren't the Fairy Princess that fits perfectly into the glass slipper of life? (But I get it, if you've been swept off your feet...it won't matter that your stilettos are made of glass, right?)

The truth is, eventually you must walk. If you're trying to walk in a glass stiletto or slipper, sooner or later it's going to shatter. LIFE (that infamous 4-letter word) has a way of doing this to all of us, especially when you're a mover and a shaker, and you're running the race of your life.

So, what do you do with all those fragmented, jagged pieces? Most seem to fall into one of two categories. Either you will be/remain the victim and continue to feel the daily pain of walking on what's shattered, or you will attempt to "fix" yourself because you see yourself as *broken*.

One way or the other, women tend to do this over and over again. Either by becoming fearful of relationships; a man-hater; a busy, stressed out, overachiever that's in and out of therapy and/or the relationships that landed her there in the first place; the one searching for the glue she defines as "Mr. Right" (or "Mr. Right Now"); or the woman who stops dreaming because she no longer believes that *she is possible*.

No matter what the resultant behavior, the motivating force is one of trying to fix what you believe is "wrong" or attempting to be something *more* because you believe that you're not enough. Thus, spending years or even a lifetime looking for "the fix" that will make you better.

I know exactly how this feels. I was this woman for many years.

With nearly half of all marriages ending in divorce, and the possibility of heartbreak everywhere we turn, is *true love* possible? Or may I say, is it probable you will meet the perfect match, be in a successful relationship, and live out a love story that continues into the sunset?

Is there such a thing as *the perfect match*? Are we looking for something (or someone) that doesn't exist? Or does it exist, but not where (or in whom) we thought it did?

Our childhood stories teach us that sooner or later *he* will come to our rescue, and be the hero of our *happily ever after*. Magically *he* will make our dreams come true.

What if it doesn't happen?

Devastating, right?

What's devastating isn't whether or not it *happens,* but that we believed it was ever *meant* to happen in the first place. It's the *idea* that this is how the *happily ever after* is "supposed" to be! The disturbing reality is that young women (and men) make plans for their lives based on these misleading, oftentimes unconscious, beliefs.

This heroic, seemingly romantic notion is quite simply not real. Period. To put this type of expectation on the "Prince" or the "Princess" is not only deceptive, but a disaster waiting to happen. Not to mention, assuming that this is every woman's fairytale is equally as destructive.

ONE relationship will NOT make your dreams come true, unless it's with the One who gave you the dreams in the first place, as well as the dreamer herself!

On the contrary, one relationship can destroy both your dreams and the dreamer. If you're missing vital relationships *within* you, the likelihood of choosing a *wrong* relationship outside of you increases dramatically. This can rob years of your happy life. Trust me, I know all too well.

What if you find yourself experiencing something that isn't part of your "ideal" love story? Or you're in the midst of a crisis that you never thought would happen to you; how do you put your life back together? How do you find YOU again in the midst of all the pain, chaos, and confusion?

Divorce isn't necessarily the answer. The illusion that "he is the wrong guy," or that "someone else will fulfill you," is dangerously misleading. If, in fact, you married the *wrong* guy, then it's time to ask yourself, "Why?" The first place to start is by getting to know the *right* girl within you.

Sure, there are a lot of post-divorce support systems out there. Yes, I tried several of them. The problem is, "getting through it" (the problem or symptoms) doesn't mean you've dealt with, and healed the core cause of your suffering.

Please hear me when I say this, just because you are in a promising new relationship doesn't mean the old one is in your past.

Pain is not your problem, and making it go away is not the cure. The cause of the pain IS the problem. HE is not your problem either. I know that may not be easy to hear. Both are symptoms of a greater cause. Really!

Even in the case where two people meet and are seemingly "perfect" for each other, there is no such thing as a perfect person, so perfect relationships cannot exist.

What *does* exist are *perfectly imperfect* people, looking for someone to join them in this mysterious adventure called LOVE/LIFE. The best relationships are not the ones that are discovered, but instead they are the ones created by those who are willing to put in the time to build something amazing with what they uncover, in themselves, each other, and the relationship.

This all begins within you...your heart. It starts with the dating relationship you have with yourself. It's the connection between your head + heart, while allowing your healthy heart to lead. The relationship between your heart and soul is the most vital part of you being authentically YOU.

Learning about the *perfectly imperfect one* feeling the pain, and living the problem is a start. Loving *her* to completion is the path that leads to healing the cause of not only your pain, but unlocking the pleasure of living in your brilliant presence.

> If divorce is IN you, then it's not in your past, nor does it stay out of your present or future.

Divorce penetrates your present at levels that are often unconscious, and has a way of producing duplicate results in your future.

Don't be fooled! The reason you divorced isn't simply because you married the wrong person. Perhaps it's because you never discovered all that was right within you, and became fully engaged to YOU before becoming engaged to another.

CHAPTER 2

THE *DISENGAGEMENT* SYNDROME

My divorce(s) happened long before I ever said, "I do" and got married. They were simply the result of a disconnected, disengaged head + heart, and the illusion that somehow the classic "love story" would make my life (or me) complete.

Why do we do what we do? There are so many reasons! We are programmed by life: the messages coming in, voices inside our heads, and the words we (and everyone else) hear coming out of our mouths. They translate into many mixed messages by what we see, hear, and do. Or what we say, and what we do not say. These messages become beliefs that guide our thoughts, words and actions. Ultimately, and oftentimes unconsciously, creating a life that is either congruent (or not) with our truest desires.

What if your desires have been based on what you *think* you want?

> Is an unconscious want the same as a conscious desire?

No.

If your beliefs and desires are not congruent, you will eventually find yourself in the destination of your beliefs (conscious or not). This leads to more want and need. The result is a state of mind and motivation that is never enough, nor satisfied.

Then what? You can either change your beliefs or desires. The choice is yours. The power is yours.

The countless reasons women feel as though they don't have time for themselves, or can't take care of themselves, are endless. I see it all the time, and unfortunately it's usually when I'm at my practice, attentively listening to a woman who is explaining to me exactly where she hurts or that she is tired and broken (physically, mentally, spiritually, or financially).

It's also in the stories I've heard as I listen empathetically to a woman's voice, interrupted with tears and a faint hint of regret, when she shares the story of the day she was diagnosed with cancer. Quickly followed by trying desperately to explain why she never seemed to have time to take care of herself, until now.

I have heard every story imaginable, and they are often riddled with stress, fear, *overwhelmedness*, busyness, bitterness, blame, shame, and/or *unforgiveness*. Many times these are echoed by an attempted explanation of, "This is just how I am. I am a worrier by nature," or "I just don't have time to take care of me."

Quite frankly it's an epidemic in our society, and it's not a diagnosis that can be fixed with a drug and/or surgery that promises a cure. Incurable simply means curable from within, and it starts by realizing that you are not "without" anything that you *need* to respond to life. The healer is the one standing in front of the mirror staring deeply into your soul.

That's right. The one answer you have been looking for doesn't show up in the form of a handsome *date*, but from within the very person that is looking back at you when you stand in the reflection of your life. It's you, my friend.

You are the answer to the vital questions you are brave enough to ask yourself. Within you are the answers that will dispel the cultural myths that convince you that you don't have enough time, what you need, or that you are not enough.

When you come to the divine revelation that you have the power to make a change, my hope is that you will also realize that you are not only part of the cause of the problem, but also a vital part of the solution. You are the answer.

Are you willing to ask the questions?

Are you willing to be the *full* reflection of the *whole* human that you are?

Are you willing to allow *you*, and your life, to be the answer to the questions you ask?

Despite not having more female role models to teach us how to be successfully single, dating, or married, it is possible. And while countless women are not living their dreams, there are many women who are.

For many of us, though, we find ourselves going through the motions. Disengaged.

CHAPTER 3

THE *SUPERWOMAN* SYNDROME

I grew up with parents who started dating at fifteen, got married at seventeen, and had their first of three children at nineteen. They were happily married for almost fifty-four years, until together "in death" they departed.

So why couldn't I find lasting love? What seemed like it would be my "Happily Ever After" eluded me for my entire adult life. That is, until I learned the secret to "Happy."

Divorce wasn't in my family, vocabulary, plan, or fairytale. Or was it?

Ever since I was fifteen years old I've had a boyfriend, husband(s), or been healing from an ex-husband (I don't like that word, so I will kindly refer to them as "WASbands" – thank you, Dr. Kay!). I spent years of my life searching for "the one," chasing an "ideal," or wondering if HE had noticed ME. Always hoping that perhaps the elusive fantasy that "it IS meant to be" would finally be.

Each time I got divorced, it was as if a piece of me was being ripped away. It left me feeling at such an intense loss; a loss of words, a loss of direction, a loss of who I was. That's because divorce is not only something that happens to couples.

Divorce is "disconnection, division, disunion, separation" (to name a few). I believe the reason it happens so frequently is because it is simply a symptom of a greater cause. That cause is the divorce or disconnection that's oftentimes deep within us. Yes, a divorce of the heart and soul. No one is immune to it.

The pain was unlike anything I had ever felt. It was a pain that pierced so deeply, and was so razor sharp that no tears, anything, or anyone could take it away. I remember telling a friend, "If I took medication, this would definitely be one of those times I would be taking drugs." I now know why people turn to drugs (prescribed or otherwise), alcohol, or "rebound" relationships to help stop the pain. I even got so desperately into my despair at one point, that I was almost willing to take my own life to stop the pain. (Now, I did say "almost willing"—thank God I was not, and did not!) To someone who has never felt this kind of pain, you are probably thinking, "That sounds totally crazy. I would never do that." Well, I never thought I would think those thoughts and be divorced either, especially not three times!

Each of my marriages left similar, yet different wounds in my heart. The devastation of betrayal, abandonment, and the "fairy tale" turned into a nightmare, left me spinning out of control. On the outside I appeared to be together, yet on the inside I was completely broken. I had been knocked off the white horse that I imagined would carry me into the sunset (my Happily Ever After) with my "Prince Charming." I didn't know where to turn, or who to trust for help.

I was ashamed, brokenhearted, and felt completely alone. The first time I told no one, except my Mom (only after three years of crying myself to sleep almost every night because my husband had told me that he wasn't sure if he wanted to be married anymore). I only told my Mom after finding out that it wasn't that he didn't want to be married, but it was that he would rather be in a relationship with someone else—the person with whom he was already having an affair.

The weeks, months and years that passed were filled with a lot of anger, blame, *unforgiveness*, pain, shame, guilt, and searching to make such an injustice okay in my mind and heart. I jumped right into another dating relationship (only to find out, unbeknownst to me, that he not only had a wife, but also another girlfriend). What!?!

I continued to seek my answers in countless bad relationships, and working excessively. I even turned to food to help ease my pain. Waking up in the middle of the night to eat a bagel with peanut butter and jelly and/or a huge bowl of chocolate ice cream was not uncommon. For the first time in my life I not only carried the intense weight of a broken heart, but the heaviness of excessive weight. I remember gaining almost fifteen pounds in less than a month—my pants went up three sizes! For the first time in my life I was over my normal, healthy weight. I didn't know what to do! Of course, being a health professional and fitness instructor, I knew how to take off the weight. However, I didn't know how to access the ability to do so. It was deeply buried in the heaviness of my pain and suffering.

People look at me and think that I know nothing about what it feels like to be overweight. Believe me, I know how it feels. I was not only gaining weight, but I was overtaken by a heaviness I didn't understand, and was seemingly losing everything I thought I knew. I felt completely out of control for the first time in my life.

It took me almost an entire year to release the extra weight, and it took me almost twelve years to let go of the extra baggage that led to continued heartache and pain. The weight loss only came after I had found the courage within myself to finally want to forgive him, "the other woman," and myself.

My prayer for almost an entire year was, "Dear God, please help me want to forgive…" Then it progressed to, "Dear God, help me to forgive." It took me a lot longer to come to the realization that it was finally time to forgive myself, and time to stop asking, "Why me?" And when I did, I was miraculously released from the boulder that I had been carrying around."

Husband number two comes into the picture after this, and I am certain that "he is the one." After a whirlwind romance, I got married again, only to experience a pain that I never dreamed I would ever have to live through again. Betrayal. And yes, Divorce Number Two. Yet I also discovered a source of strength deep within me that I never thought was possible.

The only benefit of having been through divorce before was I knew that even though I felt like I was going to die, I would in fact live through the unfathomable and make it out on the other side. But the pain cut my heart wide open, and the horrific agony left me completely and utterly exhausted. Somehow I kept it together on the outside, even though for an entire year-and-a-half I cried out to God every night while sitting on the floor of my tear-soaked closet.

Although it took me a long time to completely unleash her, there was some unexplainable warrior essence on the inside of me that would not let this thing take everything I had worked so hard to build. I was determined to keep going.

I became afflicted with the "Superwoman Syndrome" of constantly running, running, running, but getting nowhere. I simultaneously launched two businesses in a completely new state where I only knew four people, besides my young daughter. I was completely and positively in one of the biggest races of my life—the race for survival.

For several years I ran in circles, while getting nowhere, except more fatigued and deeper in debt, all the while driven by this need to succeed. Yes, during this time there were more unsuccessful dating relationships that once again were unfulfilling and disappointing. Each one of these solidified the unconscious belief that I was unlovable and that a loving, lasting relationship was not possible for me.

I was not enough, and neither was my life, no matter how hard I pushed myself. By then I had completely disengaged from my heart, while living primarily in my head. My days were filled with long lists of "To Do's" and an endless supply of "shoulds."

CHAPTER 4

THE *POOR ME* SYNDROME

Many times in the past I remember saying, "I don't feel alone...I just feel so *by myself*," and it was overwhelming. It didn't feel good. This led to my unconscious attempts to mask the pain by seeking the "perfect relationship," all while creating an overwhelming life that kept me distracted enough to be numb to the feeling of the "by-myself-ness" that plagued me. I did this by spinning more plates than an entire team of expert plate spinners/jugglers. It came from an unconscious belief that if I could live a life that felt much larger than me, then perhaps I wouldn't feel so solely me.

At least this is how I saw or explained it once I stopped long enough to step inside my heart, instead of outside of it, and really allowed myself to see what was happening.

As I continued to live my personal nightmare of heartache and shame, I also valiantly told my "Poor Me" story. It kept me in a disengaged, disempowered state of being. While all along I unconsciously believed that there was nothing I could do about it. Although God knows I tried!

The picture that I once held in my heart as the woman I was, had succumbed to the new belief that perhaps she no longer existed. I began to question if my dreams were possible, and wonder if "I" was possible. I became afraid, stuck, and unable to follow through with what I set out to accomplish in pretty much all areas of my life.

Sure, on the outside I appeared to have it together. I looked successful. I could put on a happy face when needed. Actually, I became masterful at "choosing happy." But I knew the truth. I felt and saw the pieces where no one was looking, and I told myself that it was because of this or that, and "they just didn't understand."

Poor me.

It was as if I had been put in a holding pattern, and was not only completely out of fuel, but unfortunately unable to land. I continued to circle my life, hovering from above, totally unhappy with what I was witnessing. But at least I was circling above, and not below it. Or so I thought. Later, I realized that I had in fact, been in this holding pattern since my first divorce. Ouch!

Barely keeping my head above water, and totally exhausted, I entered into another relationship that quickly became another marriage. It didn't take long before I realized that my marriage was failing once again. After over a year of an all too familiar pain and suffering, as I continued to attempt to stop the inevitable, I finally relented and surrendered to my heart.

I will never forget when God gently reminded me that if I wanted my life to be different, I must quit using my circumstantial story to justify where I was.

As long as we justify where we are, we will not move beyond there. A *Poor Me Story* will keep you poor!

A Poor Me Story *will keep you poor!*

THE POSSIBILITY

CHAPTER 5

MY (YOUR) *RICH ME* STORY OF TRUTH

Happiness can be searched for, chosen, or created. I chose to begin the creative process of healing my heart and creating my *happy ever after.*

My life changed when I told my story from the perspective of the writer, and not the character. I no longer chose to be the *Damsel in Distress*, while pretending to be the powerful *Leading Lady*. Instead, I *became* the Leading Lady in my own story, while living a new role of love, life, lessons, and legacy. This new storyteller no longer pretends to be anything that she is not. Nor does she tell a story that she doesn't choose to live.

The life-changing scene began in South Africa, while driving through the bush on a cold, moonlit July night, surrounded by some of the most magnificent, wildly free creatures I had ever seen. Super. Natural.

It was then that an overwhelming peace came over me. As I looked up into the sky, it was as if I could see the face of God looking back at me with a smile. Not only did I know that everything would be okay, but I also sensed that somehow this pain that I had been feeling would not be in vain. I knew that my story was not unique, and there were other women just like me that were in need of the peace and *knowing* that I felt. It was in that moment that I knew everything was going to be okay, and my inner "Warrior Princess" truly believed it.

Upon returning home, I learned that one of my favorite patients was dying of cancer, and I went to comfort him and his family. As I stood around his hospital bed, surrounded by his closest family, we watched him take his last breath.

Life took on a whole new meaning for me. Life is so much more than the air we breathe. It was then that I realized that we don't come into this world alone, and we don't leave it alone. The quality of our lives is measured by how much we allow the loved ones in our lives to actually be a part of our beginnings and endings, as well as the *in-betweens*.

As I held his grieving widow in my arms, I realized that love hurts sometimes, and holding onto the suffering only delays healing. After watching my own relationship dying for the past year, and fighting for love and attention, I knew it was time to let it go.

It was then that I made the conscious decision that "this time it's going to be different!" I made up my mind that if my heart was going to be broken completely open once again, this time I was going to take whatever steps necessary to not just go through divorce and a broken heart, but to truly GROW through it.

I determined in my heart that I wouldn't be afraid of the pain or desperately try to make it stop, but I would press in as needed to get to the cause of it and heal completely. I also committed to being totally open to KNOW some things about me that I hadn't been able to recognize in the past.

While driving home from my patient's funeral, I cried out to God...again. But this time, for the first time, I humbled myself enough to reach out to someone besides God for help. This is where my journey of restoration began. God answered. I listened.

The *nowhere* that my prior race had taken me to, I now refer to as my *know-where* or *somewhere*—a place without a race. It's the best kept secret; a familiar place of knowing and growing. I am beyond grateful to have made the discovery.

It's the home that is my heart, and home IS where the heart is. It's along a quiet, mysterious, windy road that appeared to be going nowhere at first, but has proven to be an adventure in and of itself—one that has allowed me to explore and discover what it means to take the road less traveled. This time I do not travel it *by myself*, but *with myself*.

Truly getting to know me through the process of *dating myself* allowed me to finally see and feel myself as a whole. It also allowed me to love myself enough to be with me in spite of my pain.

Being single, while learning to date ME, has not been an easy skill to master. (Dating a tough woman like myself has had its unique challenges!) But it has also been/is one of the best experiences of my life. The lessons I've learned are invaluable and have taught me to not only *Date Myself*, but to *Date Myself Well!*

It's worth it.

What's the price paid for a neglected, mistreated, disconnected heart and soul? It's one that's higher than you or I can pay, and the loss affects not only us, but also women (and men) everywhere. It becomes a life unimagined—an unconscious existence that affects everyone.

What then can be the benefit, and the incredible treasure of a heart and soul recognized, liked, loved, and embraced with full engagement?

Love.

Life.

Love is not only the most excellent way, it's the only way to infinite value and a life well lived. It IS life! It's life well loved and LOVE well lived. It's the place you've always dreamed you could go—the *Love of Your Life*.

Thank you for allowing me to teach you what I've learned, and now know. It's my privilege and honor to share my story with you, and the following truths and steps that will lead you to your greatest love…life.

THE LIFE-CHANGING SOLUTIONS (TRUTHS) I LEARNED THE HARD WAY:

For me it was the paralyzing effect of divorce that seemed to be the problem in my life, and the pain that kept me from moving forward in my life. The more I attempted to "undo" my divorce, the more it led me to repeating the decisions and patterns of behavior that led to more broken relationships. This is what happens when we focus on the past. It repeats itself in the future.

It wasn't until I came to the humbling truth that although I had broken relationships in my past and *felt* brokenhearted, I didn't need fixing. It was then that I truly began to heal. I also discovered that although I *felt* broken, I didn't need to live my life broken and broke. Although I was single, it didn't require a solution.

TRUTH #1: YOU DON'T NEED FIXING. (AND NEITHER DOES YOUR RELATIONSHIP STATUS.)

In the process of openly and honestly embracing my intense emotions, I was able to discover that divorce was merely the effect of a deeper disconnection between my head and heart.

This solution wasn't going to be found in a new relationship with another man (the "right" man). If I continued to allow myself to blame my present relationship status on anyone (including me), it would only perpetuate the lie that I needed someone else to complete me. This is definitely the myth that so many single/divorced women (humans) buy into. We believe that it's in another person that we will find happiness, or that we need someone else to take care of us to be happy.

I've got news for you. If you're not willing to take care of you, no one else will be either—at least not at the level that your heart deeply desires. Worse yet, you will continue to attract people into, and create circumstances in, your life that will keep you very busy tending to others' needs because you are desperately looking for someone to take care of yours.

TRUTH #2: WHEN YOU ARE WILLING TO TAKE CARE OF YOU, YOU WILL BE TAKEN CARE OF.

What I also discovered was that it wasn't going to be from me learning how to be a better person, better wife, better woman, or better anything that would heal me. Oh my goodness, the time and money I have spent on one self-help seminar after another trying to *fix* myself or make me *better*. I cannot tell you how many tens of thousands of dollars I've spent on "programs" over the years! It seemed as though every time I felt most desperate there was always another "Miracle Step-By-Step Program" promising to fix my partner, fix me, fix my relationship, make me better, make me happier, make me more money, or MORE of anything and everything I *thought* I needed for happiness.

I even approached God this way. My prayers were a laundry list of needs that I felt must be met for me to get what I wanted or felt I needed. I will never forget the day I realized that I didn't need to get what I wanted to be happy, but instead my joy would come from knowing what I truly desired.

Who knew it could come from within?

TRUTH #3: YOU DON'T NEED TO GET WHAT YOU WANT TO BE HAPPY. KNOWING WHAT YOU DESIRE WILL INSPIRE HAPPINESS.

It was when I stopped trying to get something from the outside that I tapped into truths on the inside that became my roadmap to the life I truly desired.

As I began to go deeper into my heart, I found that I had never really dealt with the pain of my first divorce. Although I had forgiven him, the other woman, and me, I had not tended to the little girl within me that needed my care and attention, unconditional love, and the priority of my time. I had gotten so caught up in my life and everyone in it that I had forgotten about *her*.

This wasn't going to happen if I continued to play the role of a victim. As I constantly told my very subtle story of "Poor Me," I got poorer and poorer. Every time I spoke of my current marital status of "divorced," I felt the need to give a quick synopsis of why I was divorced. Again, as long as I allowed myself to believe that my "why" was because of someone else, I continued to overlook the truth that perhaps my heart's cry was coming from an unanswered call, not a missed one!

I went inside my heart and into a deeper relationship with God/Jesus (not as a religion, but as a real and very tangible access into everything I believed and why, as well as everything I needed…True Love). This led me to discover many of the truths that set me free to be the happy, successful woman (and little girl) I am today, and have helped countless women and men that I've coached along the way.

The moment I heard a still, quiet voice coming from within my heart completely changed everything for me, "Shannon, do you love YOU?"

Quite honestly, I was completely taken aback. I was speechless. I sat there not knowing what to say. My mouth was wide open and my mind, no matter how hard I tried, couldn't spit out the words that I knew I wanted to say, "Yes?" So instead, I said nothing. I remember thinking, "Why is God asking me this?" (To anyone else I would have said, "Yes" with no hesitation and really thought that I meant it.) The thought of "He must know something I don't know, and of course, I don't want to tell Him something that's not true…" flooded my brain.

When God asks a question like that, it takes on a whole new meaning. I couldn't speak with words or even think of how to respond. My mind was everywhere, "Why is He asking me this? He knows everything. Do I love myself? Why can't I respond right now? What does He mean 'love'? Oh my goodness, why can't I say anything right now? Is it yes? Is it no? Of course it's not, 'No'…I think. Why can't I say anything right now?" It felt as though time stood still, a very long "*still*".

As I sat there in the quiet of the early morning, stunned and without words, I was able to mutter the simple question of, "God, why can't I answer You?"

Then I heard such a sweet, encouraging voice in my spirit. "It's okay, Shannon. In order to love you, you must get to know you. In order to get to know you, you must spend time with you. It's okay."

Wow. I felt so relieved. Peaceful. He also showed me that in order for me to get what I desire, it was necessary to stop pursuing or accepting that which I did not. So I asked what I could do. He gently whispered, "Date Yourself."

He then reminded me that He is Love and since He is in me and I am in Him…I was already IN LOVE.

TRUTH #4: LOVE IS IN YOU.

Could it be the love that I had been seeking in men, including my relationship with God, was already in me, and all I needed to do was receive it by engaging with my heart, and the little girl, little boy, and adult woman in it?

This is when I began to date myself…*well.* I fully committed to my heart, and the relationship I had with myself. I stopped pursuing everything and everyone else, and for the first time in my life I began pursuing me. I received the love that was/is me by fully engaging with me for no other reason but to love me. I didn't do it to get anything or anyone. I began to love me with no conditions. Unconditionally.

I also stopped trying to be better or even be my best. Better requires comparison to others, the past, or some ideal future. Best implies that somehow all versions of me aren't acceptable, except the version of "best." I remember thinking, "Who defines best anyway?"

This is BEST. You being at your *best* is you being the truest version of yourself. You being authentically you *is* your best, and that can look very different on any given day.

Personally, I define B.E.S.T. as "Being Excellent Starting Today." The most excellent way is LOVE...true love...the method that never fails. Best is being fully engaged with the love that's in you, the love that is you. This is the way to BE. Being Engaged (with love) Starting Today.

Oh, and by the way, the whole notion of *better than* can become a dangerous trap when you date you or anyone else. Just because you are *better than* before doesn't mean you're *being* healthfully, *excellently* you...in love. The question is, "Are you being fully engaged with who you are now?" Also, just because *he* is *better than* your last date doesn't mean he is best for you. (You got it?)

TRUTH #5: WHEN YOU ENGAGE
IN THE LOVE THAT'S IN YOU,
YOU WILL BE IN LOVE.
(Do you still need to be convinced?)

Are you ready to fully engage in BEING you and *dating yourself well?* Are you currently living your dreams? Are you actively expressing your creative nature and contributing your creativity to those around you, and the world as a whole?

You must be with someone who is going to inspire you to be the most inspiring person you can be. This doesn't happen if you are living a life of quiet desperation, due to a yearning for more, while having an unwillingness to inspire your*self*. That someone you have been searching for is YOU!

Dating yourself does not mean that you will never date again. It doesn't mean that you must be single for the rest of your life or divorced, nor does it mean that if you marry, you have to stop dating YOU! It also does not mean that you *do not* desire to fall in love, and even marry in the future.

Dating yourself means that you are willing to pursue *her*, spend time getting to know *her*, listen to *her*, nurture and care for *her*. It means making the commitment to become one with *her* for the rest of your life. Learning to date yourself well is about having a sacred relationship, filled with love and life, with YOU for a lifetime!

Whether you're single or married, you can live life with a single-minded focus of loving YOU until "*death do YOU part.*"

It's a time for you to be more than "taken," but fully received by you.

TRUTH #6: WHAT YOU'VE BEEN LOOKING FOR IS NOT ONLY IN YOU, BUT IT IS YOU!

She has been quietly waiting to be recognized, noticed, and approached. She is waiting to be invited to join you on an adventure that is not only romantic and mysterious, but is also majestic. She will be the best *date* you'll ever have and your union with her will inspire you to love (and live), like never before.

I am here to encourage you today and remind you that your purpose in the world is not that of just being someone's (__fill in the blank__), but your purpose for being on planet earth is far greater.

You are here to be profoundly and simply YOU. You are commissioned for a very special purpose that is "uniquely you." It's in you. It is the rhythm of your soul, or your heart's song that has sung since before you were born and will continue on in harmony after you pass. It is that still small voice that cries out to you…pay attention, notice me, love me, nurture me so I can become all that I am designed and destined to be. It's the desire to sing with every fiber of your being, and share the creative message that is fully present deep within you.

It IS you!

We as women have become distracted and out of tune long enough. We have not only lost our focus on the mission at hand, but we have gotten off-course. Our lives have somehow become more about what we think we *should* be doing, instead of passionately pursuing that which we would love to be doing and loving. We have become so focused on taking care of everything and everyone on the outside, we have forgotten about one of the most important relationships. It's the inner relating with the person that we are.

This is the only thing that will allow us to truly love others and serve our purpose.

I've got great news for you. There is no such thing as "single," except when you recognize the human creation as all being part of a greater "ONE". This is the only "single" that exists. Individual, yes; alone, no!

Ladies, you only *think* you are single or alone. We are all part of a greater creation, a bigger picture, a grander vision, and a divine connectedness. The female nature has a more powerful role in this masterpiece than ever before in our history.

> *Our deepest fear is not that we are inadequate. Our deepest fear is that we are powerful beyond measure. It is our light, not our darkness that most frightens us. We ask ourselves, 'Who am I to be brilliant, gorgeous, talented, fabulous?' Actually, who are you not to be? You are a child of God. Your playing small does not serve the world. There is nothing enlightened about shrinking so that other people won't feel insecure around you. We are all meant to shine, as children do. We were born to make manifest the glory of God that is within us. It is not just in some of us; it's in everyone. And as we let our own light shine, we unconsciously give other people permission to do the same. As we are liberated from our own fear, our presence automatically liberates others."* —Marianne Williamson

The date that changed my life forever was the day that I finally acknowledged *the hard*, and *the pain* in my life, and instead of running from it, I embraced it and learned a new way, another way. You've heard about the "worse," now allow me to share with you the "better," and as I've said, there is something better than "better" and quite honestly, it's not even "best." It's a new way. It's an excellent way; the excellence of YOU BEING IN LOVE WITH YOU.

It's giving *you* permission; permission to stop. Stop trying to be better, get better, or look for better. That's what *dating yourself well* is all about. It's permission to GO. To go *BE* the mission—your mission.

Are you willing to be the one who sweeps you off your feet long enough for you to get the perspective you need in order to see through the broken glass in your life? Are you ready to be the loving partner of your soul? Are you prepared to discover the little princess inside you and allow her to be the creative, powerful queen of your heart?

Never before in our history has it been a better time to be a woman. The world is waiting for you!

Until you get your basic needs of true love and acceptance met, you will always feel a yearning for more. You can look for it outside of yourself as you seek it from others, or by chasing success, fame, or money. The truth is, there are no substitutes that will satisfy your thirst. Only discovering YOU and the love inside you, and then authentically being YOU will bring satisfaction, significance, and substance to your life. Love finds you from the inside, out.

TRUTH #7: WHEN YOU BECOME WILLING TO KNOW AND LOVE YOU FOR YOU AND NO ONE ELSE, YOU WILL TRULY FIND LOVE— AND IT WILL FIND YOU.

When I discovered this truth, I found love, and true love found me!

You may be wondering, "Is this really possible?" The answer is a resounding, "YES."

Here's how you can fall in love, fully engage in your life, and live the life you LOVE.

Dating Yourself Well is the key to healing not only your heart, but also your head, soul, body, spirit, and emotions. This benefits you, as well as humanity as a whole.

I have discovered the mystery behind living an engaging life of love, and it's no longer a secret. It's a choice, and there is a proven, effective path to follow.

Before you choose, I would like to make a very important announcement. Dating yourself for any reason other than to get to know and love you (for example: secretly or not so secretly doing it because you think it will help you *attract* "Mr. Right") is still *conditional* love. If your desire is to be loved unconditionally, then it starts with you.

Are you willing to date and love yourself with no conditions or strings attached? Are you willing to be 100% accessible and emotionally available to you? Are you willing to be the best date you've ever had? Are you willing to fully engage in your life?

If the answer is yes, I will show you how. Now.

Congratulations.

WELL...Come!

I will be here with you every step of the way.

Over the next twelve weeks we will meet together by going through the following *Five Engagements of a Great Lover* and *Seven Engagements of a Great Life*. I will show you how to increase your ability to love. You will *Date Yourself Well* with Weekly Dates that allow you to become fully engaged and fall in LOVE with YOU from the inside, out. I suggest you get a favorite journal and title it your *Date Book*. Keep it with you while you read, and during each of your dates.

THE PROCESS

FIVE ENGAGEMENTS OF A GREAT LOVER

MEET YOU
KNOW YOU
VALUE YOU
BE YOU
LOVE YOU!

CHAPTER 6

ENGAGEMENT ONE – *MEET YOU*

Show up as the great lover of your life.

Show up.

If you don't, who will? The engaged few show up, and share what they know. The disengaged masses do not. My boxing trainer, a former Champion Boxer, says 80 percent of his success was due to simply showing up. Many want to be in a Ring of Champions when everyone is watching, but few emerge when no one is looking. If you want to be engaged, show up in the ring every day. Don't wait for someone to "put a ring on it."

As with any relationship, there are essential phases you must go through. The great love you create within yourself starts as other great relationships begin. The first of twelve essential engagements to *Dating Yourself Well* is quite simply, *The Meeting*.

The first step in a relationship is meeting someone. You must show up. Whether this is in person, over the phone, Internet, or in your imaginative mind known as an *idea*. Am I the only one who has ever fallen in love with the idea of someone? That potential, or possibility, of the person he *could* or *should* be.

Now you may be thinking this is a bit silly because you are a grown woman, and your mind is saying, "Of course I have met me." I thought I had "met me" too, but I had met only versions of me or the *idea* of me. The person I thought I was, or *should* be, or who others thought I was, or *should* be.

It wasn't until I sifted through all the roles, responsibilities, labels, and lists that I finally found out I am more than the sum of my many pieces. When I was stripped of all I was hiding behind, and underneath, what I found was very different from what I had once imagined. Suddenly I was seeing my exposed heart for the very first time, and it was gloriously gorgeous.

It's the moment when you see yourself eye-to-eye, face-to-face, and heart-to-heart. It's the moment you finally recognize you, and in that transcending acknowledgment, the earth seemingly stops revolving for a second (or longer). You have not only been seen, but you have been noticed. Yes, you are consciously aware of your own presence, and it is incredibly powerful. You are magnetically attractive, and you feel it.

Essentially this is when you locate yourself, and you take time to specifically pay attention to the woman that is right here, right now. *She* is present, and you are profoundly aware of your presence. This is when your head (what it thinks of you) and your heart (what it knows of you) come together and acknowledge one another.

Until you consciously meet you, it's impossible to date you.

Prior to meeting anyone important, you may feel a little anxious, or perhaps even a bit awkward. That's okay, you are about to meet someone that you will be spending the rest of your life with. You're entitled to feel however you want to feel right now. By the way, how are you feeling?

We have meetings every day; some good, and some not so good. While many are planned, and scheduled, many are not. But usually the meeting is with someone outside of us. And we ask ourselves questions like,"Am I prepared? Do I look okay? What will I say? Will they accept me? Does that person like me? Was I noticed? Does any of this matter? Heck, do *I* matter?" And the questions go on for days. It can become mind boggling to say the least. Then there are all the rules, or socially acceptable ways to meet, greet, and possibly stay in touch. God forbid if you ask too many questions, and perhaps appear to be "too into someone."

Don't worry. Be yourself!

Every expert will tell you that in order to be successful in relationships, and in life, you must be yourself. That's great advice. However, it's based on the assumption that you KNOW WHO YOU ARE. This is for many the one thing that's missing. Most people do not know who they really are. I know this sounds odd, but it has been my experience, as I have cared for and coached thousands of people over almost three decades. It has become very apparent that not everyone knows precisely who she or he is. In fact, very few people seem to have made this incredible life-changing discovery of meeting themselves up close and personal.

Thankfully you will not be one of them. This entire process will help you to not only have this monumental meeting, but it will help you get to know *her* very well, by dating you well!

Please do not be in a hurry to go too quickly from Engagement One to Engagement Two. The best tool for making *me* fully meet me, was doing an exercise that has helped myself, and countless others to clearly see who we are, by recognizing who we are not.

It's called the *Board Meeting.* I first introduced this experience in my book, *Dr. Shannon Knows...The 12 Steps for* WELLTHY *People.* As I meet people from around the world who have read my book, the one thing that people mention most often is how much the *Board Meeting* helped them.

What it did for me personally was to expose any preconceived ideas or limiting beliefs that had been given to me throughout life about who I was NOT. It also helped me let go of those beliefs, and any negative feelings that I had toward myself, or the person they came through.

This meeting, however, is much more intimate than a *Board Meeting,* this is *your* meeting, and you can refer to it as *My Meeting.*

Before you have this very memorable meeting, I would like to equip you for it.

Unlike any other first meeting or first date, this time you will not be putting on your power suit or favorite dress, and stilettos, nor will you be taking an hour to do your hair and make-up. Instead, you will be taking it all off. *Naked and unashamed* is what I like to call it. No masks, no hiding. I want you to take a shower, or hot bath, wash all the make-up off your face, and put on your favorite pajamas. Find a comfortable, quiet place where you will not be disturbed. Or hey, stay naked, and crawl into bed with your soft, comfy blankets.

WEEK ONE
THE *NAKED AND UNASHAMED* DATE

Grab your *Date Book* and a pen. Answer the following questions: What is your name? Beyond your given name, what do you call yourself? Please be honest, have you ever called yourself a name that wasn't very loving or lovely?

If your answer is yes, *welcome to the club.* And thanks for being honest.

We've all done it.

The next, bigger question is, "Do you wish to continue to do it?" If the answer is, "No," then I applaud you and say, "Congratulations."

Whenever my clients say things to themselves that are not loving, empowering or kind, I ask them, "Who told you this?" Because usually there is some experience or someone who has caused them to believe that they are less than the brilliant, beautiful person they truly are.

Today you are going to have the opportunity get to the bottom of it, and settle this debate once and for all.

Here's where *My Meeting* comes into play. Please read through the following instructions, then proceed with your meeting in the quietness of your mind and heart.

Envision a boardroom. I want you to get a feel for what the room is like, what the table is like, how many chairs there are, where the doors are, where the windows are, if any. What color are the walls? The table?

Next, I want you to slowly invite the people into the room who have made you feel "less than", unlovable, unworthy, insignificant, afraid, and/or insecure. By making this open-invitation, you are inviting individuals you may not be consciously aware of to come and join you. You may be somewhat surprised when they show up.

As they come in, allow them to sit down at the boardroom table. One by one, they will come. Welcome them in. They may be past loves, friends, or they may be the people closest to you. They may be coworkers, relatives, or maybe even a kindergarten teacher. Whoever they are, welcome them into the room.

Now what I want you to do is this: I want you to take a moment, and go to each person individually. I want you to let them know how their words affected you. I want you to let them know how their actions have affected you. I want you to be present with each person in the moment, until you get to the point where you feel like you've said all that you need to say, felt all that you need to feel, and you are ready to forgive and release them.

When you forgive a person, move to the next one. One by one, I want you to have a conversation with every person in the room, and when you are finished, I want you to very graciously dismiss everybody from the room and thank them for coming. Release them to go on with their lives, and now release yourself to go forward with yours.

Before you leave the room, see yourself empowered with this new sense of freedom. Look deeply into the eyes of the *free woman* standing in front of you. See her clearly. What do you see? Acknowledge her. How does she feel? How do you feel about her? If necessary, forgive her. Accept all of who she is. See and feel her heart. Say what you desire to say, and feel what you feel. Fully engage with her in the moment. Embrace her. Love.

Ready? Please put down your *Date Book*. Next, sit with your hands in your lap. Palms up. Close your eyes. Take a few deep breaths, and relax your shoulders. Breathe. Take as much time as you need.

It's only you now. Begin your meeting with you.

Welcome back. How did it go? Please take time to write about your experience in your *Date Book*. Who was at your meeting? How did you feel? What did you say? How do you feel right now? Now what do you call yourself?

Dating yourself well is not about waiting to settle down, but getting settled *deep down* in your soul. Writing down every detail of what you saw, felt, and experienced at your meeting will help you do this.

CHAPTER 7

ENGAGEMENT TWO – *KNOW YOU*

Once you show, it's easy to know. After the meeting, and introduction, the next question that quickly follows is, "What do you do?" This is where you get to respond with what you *have known* or what you are *willing to know*. Respond with care. We don't see our future; we hear it. That's because we create our lives with the words we speak. What you say is what you get. Talk about your *who*, and your *do* will soon change. Your future will be created.

Often we equate who we are with what we do. Of course, your *being* is much greater than your *doing*. Yes. However, it's incredible when what you do comes from your most genuine state of being. For most, unfortunately, this is not the case, resulting in disengagement at some level. It can also perpetuate it. Many times it's the consequence of choosing to follow fear instead of the faithful call of a passionate heart. Whether this is true for you or not, please keep in mind that you are much greater than the sum of your resume.

Years ago I worked as an Executive Recruiter (a.k.a. Headhunter) for a company that placed executives in the financial industry. Every day I spoke with highly paid individuals who may, or may not be, looking for new opportunities in their field. One of the primary questions I would ask was, "What would it take for you to make a move to another company?" I cannot tell you how often I heard, "Shannon, I would take less money if you can find me a job I love." Even at that time I found myself speaking far more about desire, passion, and purpose with my clients then trying to recruit them for a position. My future destiny of being a Life Coach was calling out loud and clear, even way back then.

It's not about what you do, as much as who you are, while you're doing it. You being *you* can have many roles. So, which roles do you choose? Which roles are truly reflecting you, authentically expressed, and fully engaged?

This is your time to really get to know you. It's time for you to give yourself permission to dream again. What is it that you desire?

Often when I ask my coaching clients what they desire, quickly they respond with, "I don't know." Most are convinced that they truly don't know, or haven't yet discovered the mystery of what they desire in life. For some they knew at one time, but the pains of disappointment have convinced them that they no longer know. They lost the certainty of what they "thought they knew" because along with their disappointments and discouragements, they disengaged from their heart, and the pursuit of their dreams.

I call this a *Divorce of Heart.*

For the majority it begins along life's journey due to an event, whether it was the moment a loved one or someone of influence said that you couldn't do it, or you were silly to believe you ever could. Those moments happen in life, yet still there is a voice that whispers or cries from within your heart saying, "Yes I can."

Then there are others' voices, circumstances, disappointments, betrayals that come into your life and confirm this original message of, "No, you cannot." The head is saying "no," while the heart desperately wants to hold on to the hope of "yes." Perhaps you have heard these voices. We all have at one time or another.

The more we hear it, the more we see it, and the more we see it, the more we believe it. This deceptive, and often unconscious, belief perpetuates a vicious cycle that disrupts the song of desire within our hearts. It does so by programming our thoughts, words, and actions that become contrary to our dreams.

That which we love deep within our hearts begins to hurt too much to continue believing, and engaging with it. So we begin to disengage (divorce) from our heart and turn our attention elsewhere. And the race is on. This race leads to detours, and many dead-ends and self-made deadlines. Each one adding to the pain of the past one, until one day we wake up and we wonder. Where am I? How did I get here? Who am I? Why am I here? We feel as though we know nothing, but are seeking everything while no longer knowing what the "one thing" (that seems to be the KEY) truly is. We search for the key that will unlock our heart, doubting if there is such a thing. Wondering if perhaps we were wrong in ever believing that dreams really do, and can, come true.

There is fear, a sense of loss, confusion; the list of reasons why seems endless.

This leads to running from our dreams, or wrestling with the dreamer. Oftentimes battling the only one who can help us find that which we seek. It can also cause intense busy-ness that creates distraction, leading to overwhelming exhaustion. This feeling can overtake the soul, and before long we don't even know if what we once desired is even true for us any longer.

The first question to ask yourself is: Am I willing to spend some time getting to know me?

The second question to ask yourself, once again is: Am I willing to wake up and dream again?

Then ask yourself again, "When was the last time I was fully engaged with me and my life? What happened that caused me to disengage? What am I afraid of? What do I believe about myself, my fears, and the desires of my heart?"

This is a great time to take a moment and quietly contemplate where you are. It's also a gigantic opportunity to discover that perhaps there is another way to see the current life you're living. Imagine if you could view it through the lens of a creative artist or dreamer? The choice is yours. Are you willing to choose?

In any first meeting, there is the moment that you decide:

A: I like this person and would like to get to know this person better.
B: I don't like this person, and do not wish to know this person better.
C: I'm not sure how I feel, but I'm open to discovering something new.

After *meeting you*, what do you think?

If your answer is A. then write down all the things you like about *her*. If your answer is B., would you be willing to be open to a new perspective for at least the next ninety days? (You will thank me later.) If your answer is C., please allow yourself to begin to see what's possible.

Take the time to record your answers in your *Date Book*. And please do yourself a favor, graciously extend the same hope and belief to yourself that you have so often given to others. Remember in the past when you have focused more on someone's "potential" or "possibility" than what you actually saw sitting in front of you? Do the same for you. (You know what I'm talking about.)

The Know You Engagement of *Dating Yourself Well* is based on not only discovery, but also decision. It's up to you.

Once you make your decision, the best way to discover your desires is to literally, "*Dis your cover*". Really! Once again, it's what I call getting *naked and unashamed*. Here we go again, like Date One wasn't enough? Nope!

Let's face it, we live in a world (especially the dating world) where people will take their clothes off for someone they barely know, but yet they are scared to death to get naked with themselves and take a look at what's really on the inside of who they really are.

This is your time to see *you* like you've never seen yourself before. It's time to hang out with you...again.

Yes, that's right. Invest some time in getting to know you. So often we never ask ourselves the questions that we ask others when we meet them. Or we wish that others would ask us.

> The highest compliment you can give yourself is that of your own undivided attention.

Attention is defined as observant care, and acts of courtesy or devotion (as in courtship). Quite simply it's caring for the observer, an essential element in *dating yourself well.* It's also referred to as T.L.C. When we pay attention to ourselves, we tenderly, and lovingly care for ourselves.

Have you ever been on a date with someone who was very hard to talk to, or wouldn't look at you when you were speaking? Chances are there wasn't a second date.

It's so important to look at yourself when you are talking to you. I mean really allowing yourself to see and be seen by you.

Unfortunately, this isn't always easy to do. So often we look at the "potential" within others, yet fail to see "possibility" in ourselves. We are quick to point out "the facts" that confirm or explain why we are where we are, or not where we would like to be. Or we resort to the age-old deception of saying, "This is just how I am." We act as though we are just fine with how we are, but deep inside we long for something (someone) more.

How can you love yourself, while seeing yourself as unlovable?

For years this was my story. I attempted to love me, while I silently believed that I wasn't lovable. This belief led to not only several decisions ending in many personal heartaches, but continuing to chase the uncatchable.

The feeling of hopelessness leads people to look everywhere for it, or to give up and disengage from life. Either way, both lead to the same destination, a divorced heart that will show up in a myriad of problems/symptoms.

That's because hope isn't something that another can give you. It's not found on the outside of you or your circumstances.

Having worked with terminally ill cancer patients, as well as other "un-terminally well" patients in my private practice, I have witnessed how powerful hope can be in healing. In fact, it's not only powerful, but also foundational in helping people heal and live well. It's miraculous.

Hope is one of the most vital foundational cornerstones for an engaged life.

Throughout the years, many patients and coaching clients have told me that I have given them hope. Quickly I inform them that I cannot give anyone hope. I assure them that hope is something that's already within them, and a true healer merely plays the role of the one helping to awaken their hope.

Hope is more than a wishful, flippant want. Hope is a positive expectation. But it's even more than that.

Hope is your belief(s), your desire(s), and trust (who/what you trust, as well as the courage required to be vulnerable enough to trust).

Faith is the substance of this hope. So faith is the action that is manifested from it. Someone once told me that faith isn't a noun, but a verb. Then hope is both a noun and a verb. It becomes a noun once it's awakened enough to manifest itself in substance. That substance is present in the way we live our lives. It's reflected in that which we believe, desire, and trust.

The most empowering truth ever written is that when all is taken into account, "three things remain." They are faith, hope, and love, the greatest being that of love. And love is the only thing that does not fail.

If you want to succeed in *dating yourself well,* in living life well, love is the only way that does not fail. It's the chief cornerstone, and the only thing we can truly build upon.

So let's talk about love, baby.

Do you love yourself? If the answer isn't "Yes" yet, that's okay. It's going to take some time to get to know you well enough to fall in love with you. But if you are attempting to get to know you just so you can get something from you, then it's really not true unconditional love. Perhaps it's manipulation. What do I mean when I say this?

For example: You are going to spend time with you eating well and exercising only because you want you to be a certain size. I hear this all the time. If I just lose ten more pounds, then I will love myself. If I got my breasts enlarged or my face lifted, then I would love myself. I need to work on me so I can attract the right partner into my life. First of all, loving you and working on you are not the same. Spending time with you in order to fall in love with you is working *with* you. Could you be open to love you without trying to get something from you? To love you for no other reason but LOVE.

Why is it that we want someone else to love us just the way we are, but we are not willing to do it for ourselves? Why is it that we want a special someone to love us unconditionally, but what we are giving that person is only the version that we thought would be lovable?

I know this is getting deep, and probably a little uncomfortable right now. Please hang in there with me and keep reading.

What if you discovered the heart that is within you and the TRUE YOU? What if you fell in love with *her* because *she* is yours to love? What if because of that love you cared for her by tending to her needs, desires, and dreams? From that powerful and loving place, others will have the opportunity to engage with the one that is truly you. The woman that's naturally at ease because she is comfortable with the one she loves. She wants nothing from herself except to show up and be *herself*, live her purpose, and experience her dreams.

What if?

What if you didn't have to cover up and hide anymore? What if you could love yourself enough to come out from under all that stuff you use to mask your "less than" imperfections?

What if you loved yourself enough to care for you because you simply *love you?*

Imagine no longer living beneath big shirts and baggy pants because you don't feel sexy? Imagine no longer feeling like you have to dress in low necklines and high hemlines because you thought it was what "they" wanted? What do you want? More importantly, what do you desire?

Imagine no longer making excuses for what you can't do, but doing what you can? Imagine engaging in the life that you have right now with no condition that it has to get *better* for you to celebrate it?

> We will care for that which we value,
> and we will value what we love.

I have met countless women over the years that simply do not like looking in the mirror. They don't want to look, they don't like what they see, and they certainly do not want to watch themselves.

When I opened my first workout studio, I designed it so there would be a "mirror-free" zone for those who were not yet ready to see themselves in the mirror.

What I now know is that "to see" has very little to do with a mirror, and has more to do with "the she" who is looking.

Today when I'm training my clients, I purposefully put them right in front of the mirror.

The heaviness of self-hatred is oftentimes the extra weight we need to lose. Not losing the ten or twenty pounds that we are convinced will allow us to love ourselves!

Once you love yourself enough to care for you, being your healthy weight won't seem so impossible.

Perhaps your weight problem has more to do with a "wait problem."

Are you *waiting* to love (and care for) you until you lose weight or until you meet "Mr. Right" and get married, or your husband shows you more attention, or the kids are out of school? Perhaps you keeping YOU locked up inside is what's causing your weight problem. It's time to release her once and for all.

Today is your day to lose the heaviness that has been getting in the way of your undivided attention, and causing you to put your life on hold.

You can choose to either press pause or play. Which one is it going to be?

WEEK TWO
THE *GETTING DOWN* *(AND NOT SO DIRTY)* DATE

In order to *date yourself well,* you must go down under the surface of the obvious, and ask the deeper questions that only your heart can answer. Are you ready for a great week of dating?

First, let's start with the many roles you play, many times with very little joy. This week I want you to grab your *Date Book* and take time to write down everything you do in detail. This is a list of all the roles, responsibilities, or "hats" that you wear. Part of getting naked and unashamed is being able to look at all you wear, and determine if it fits in your life. I say, "If you don't love it, take it off."

This was one of the first things I did after my last (yes, I do mean LAST) divorce. I literally had several pieces of tag board and a big marker on the floor in front of me. While on my knees I filled almost two tag boards with everything I was in charge of or had a role in. It was overwhelmingly frustrating to say the least! No wonder I was feeling like I was drowning, and unable to take the life-saving breath I so desperately needed.

One by one I evaluated my every role and responsibility. As I released the ones I was no longer passionate about, or in love with, I freed myself so much that soon I was able to let go in all areas of my life. Please do this for yourself; you will be surprised at how much of your existence may be happening on "auto pilot" or "default."

You can change this, and re-engage with your life again.

By putting YOU (or what appears to be you) on paper in front of you, you will begin to see yourself in a new way. Or begin to see how you would desire to see you.

I would like to ask you a much deeper question. This is for the bold, brave woman that you are. It may seem like the Second Date is way too early to be asking these types of questions, but I did say that your First Date was not going to be a typical, ordinary date, didn't I? Well, neither are the second, third…etc.

Please take a moment right now, and take a deep breath. If you do not yet feel able to answer these questions for yourself, you can always come back during another date and do so.

"What masks do you put on each day? What masks are you still wearing, even when you are completely naked? Are you still wearing the mask of *shame*? Would you like to set these masks down?"

It is possible, dear one. As with anything we wear, we get to choose if we like how it fits, if we like how it feels, and whether or not we want to wear it again, or ever.

The greatest outfit we can put on is the garment of forgiveness, for both ourselves, and others. The undergarment of love will allow you to wear forgiveness with ease and comfort.

Take another deep breath, please. Let's talk about one more question I would like to leave you with today, and this week. Ask yourself, "What do I love to do?"

It's time to start dreaming and creating again. Create a list of "Loves" in your *Date Book*. Write down all the people and things you value, and love in your life. Include that which you love to do, and love about you.

Plan to do something this week that you love to do. Whatever it may be, put your whole heart into it. Enjoy it, and don't forget to take some pictures. I would love to see them. Picture yourself thoroughly loving and enjoying your life. Please do this, and take a picture. One can never have too many *Happy Selfies*.

Taking pictures each day has helped me, and my clients, look for daily reminders of what we're grateful for. Whatever you pay attention to will grow.

Look for inspiration in everything you do. Everywhere. A picture is worth a thousand words, and more. So are you.

CHAPTER 8

ENGAGEMENT THREE – *VALUE YOU*

Appreciate or depreciate? That is the question. Your value and worth are your greatest assets, as long as YOU recognize them. With appreciation, they increase. But with lack thereof, they depreciate over time, leading to a feeling of "less than" This "scarcity mentality" lacks value and worth. And it's certainly not a true reflection of who you are. It's the opposite of abundance and prosperity, as well as one of the most costly counterfeits.

Your greatest wealth is the *WELLTH* that's within you. How *WELLTHY* are you?

Is the *WELLTH* (your innate value) within you being fully expressed in your body, mind, spirit, and life? This is what it means to be *WELLTHY*.

Are you fully engaged with the diamond that is you?

Let's find out, shall we? You will value *you* and *your time* by truly knowing your value (dreams, desires, gifts, goals).

What is it that you love most about you, and your life? What do you desire to experience most in your life? What valuable love, wisdom, and adventures do you carry within your heart? What gift would you like to share with the world? If money were no object, what would you do? How would you contribute to the world?

Too few people ask themselves these types of questions. And without the question, the answer is far reaching. Many ask, "Why me?", while rarely considering, "Why not me?" We ask questions like, "Why am I here?" or "What next?" While fewer brave souls have answered the vital question of, "Since I am here, what am I doing now with the life/time I've been given?"

Besides the gift of life itself, and the innate value that we bring into this world, we are given two infinitely valuable commodities when we arrive.

The first is, *breath*, known as "inspiration". The second is *time*, best known as the valuable commodity we're given, but only in limited quantity, having a distinct and unknown expiration date. Outside of us time, however, is infinite. With no beginning or ending, time simply is. What we breathe into it is what gives it the greatest value.

In order to receive these gifts well, we must be able to breathe fully. Our physical and spiritual natures are directly related to this. How we breathe in the breath of life (inspiration), and breathe it out (inspire) before we expire is absolutely vital.

Yes, they affect our vitality, but so much more. They *are* vitality. Anything that affects our vitality has a direct effect on our life...time. Period.

This takes eating well, exercise, and self-care to a whole new level. It's no longer simply what you're eating that matters, but what's eating you. Research has shown that we humans take anywhere from 17,000-30,000 breaths each day. How many of your breaths are you aware of? Do you experience conscious, rhythmic breathing on a regular basis? Did you know that physical movement (or as I like to say, "playing") is a great way to give your body this gift of rhythmic breathing? So is deep breathing or yoga.

This isn't only health care I'm talking about, but *life care*.

SELF care IS the new health care.

Are you willing to take caring for you and your physical, as well as spiritual, body off your "should list"?

My decades of experience have shown me time and time again that we will care for that which we value. How valuable are you? How much do YOU value YOU, your breath, and your time?

Or are you giving yourself away? Are you giving your time away faster than it's coming in? If you don't value your time, no one else will either.

We get so busy saying "yes" to everyone else, that we feel as though we have to say "no" to that which we value most…ourselves, our health, dreams, desires, those we love.

Often my patients or coaching clients will tell me they don't have time to take care of themselves. Is time the issue or how we value it? We will talk about not having enough time, while being stressed out. Then we spend time trying to manage our stress. Perhaps we don't need to manage stress or our time. Instead, we can create peace with our time.

Consider this from a recent blog I posted called, "*Watch and See: Your New Time Peace*".

> *"T...im...e is on my side. Yes it is." Perhaps the Rolling Stones were right.*
>
> *Is it really about time management? Or is it about managing or (wo)managing the I'M in T(I'M)E?*
>
> *Perhaps even attempting to manage something as profound as time is what's speeding up the (wo)man-aging or man-aging process!*
>
> *It's time to focus not on your watch, but the woman or man who's looking at it.*

Your "I'M" has more to do with your life and time than you imagine!

I am not ON time or OUT OF time. I'M in T(I'M)E and so are you.

If you've ever noticed how relative time is, you know exactly what I'M talking about. The days go by slowly, but the years pass quickly. The minutes tick by, but the hours fly. You're early if you show up before expected, and late if you don't. Expectations, perceptions, and definitions have more to do with time than the dials on the clock.

Am I right or am I right?

Some say they are a "Morning Person" or a "Night Person." I'M quite simply a "Today" Person, learning to play in the middle of this beautiful gift called "T(I'M)E."

I remember the day I realized I didn't need to allow time to run my life anymore. It was the day that "What day?" became "Today" and "What time?" became "Now."

"How?" you ask.

Something as relative as time must be given individualized attention, because, as with anything that's relative, it's personal. It is very personal. And what if there is plenty of it, and we no longer need to stress about it or be a slave to it?

Instead, we can put our I AM into it and make peace with it once and for all...time!

Yes, it's about time! (I agree!)

What T(I'M)E is on your side, really?

Would you fully engage with it, in it, and within it? Would you allow yourself to fully DATE the date?

What is this War on Time business anyway? It's time to make Love not War! It's time to become ONE with it, until death do us part.

The answer?

Become one with the I AM that you are, and the I AM that gave it to you in the first place. Then do it well for a life...time!

If you want to do life well, live your day well.

If you want to live your day well, love it well.

If you desire to love it well, you must love the T(I'M)E you're in...loving and DATING YOU WELL!

It will love you back!

*T(I'M)E **IS** ON YOUR SIDE. **YES IT IS!***

What if you believed that time was on your side?

Oftentimes we trade our time for so many other things, including money. We also trade our health for it, because we claim we have no time because we are so busy working for money. Then we have lots of money, but no health to enjoy the time that remains. Unfortunately, even our money can't buy back time or our health.

We come into this world as gifts of love. Being love. We then *unlearn* love by no longer learning of ourselves. We learn very little, if anything, about love, how to love ourselves, as well as others, or how to build loving relationships. We lose sight of our true value and worth, so we look for it outside of ourselves. We forget about how irreplaceable we really are. We therefore attempt to substitute ourselves with unworthy replacements.

Interestingly, we also learn very little, if anything, about money. So we get educated about everything else, while going more deeply into debt. We work for money. We love money. We look for love in all the wrong places, and create unhealthy, unhappy relationships. Then get divorced, and end up losing most of our money. Broke and broken, we start the cycle again. Perhaps it's not *we* that are broken, but the cycle.

Something is desperately wrong with this picture.

The answer?

Stop re-cycling the cycle of *broken*.

Be love. Stay in love by loving God, yourself, and others (yes, in that order). Own your value and worth. Don't love money. Learn about money. Love your purpose. Work to share what you love with as many people as possible. Commit to your life's work versus work life. Give freely. Love openly. Creatively make money. Don't work for it, or trade your time for it. Discover how to teach your money to make money. You grow. Watch your money grow. Share it with others, and those who have yet to come into this world. Leave your gifts planted in the hearts, souls, and accounts of those you love and those they will love. Give an account of a life well loved, and love well lived.

This is the value of YOU...in time. Right on time. This is truth. You are not only in T(I'M)E, but YOU (okay, **U**) are in the middle of tr**U**th.

The more you know about you and your truth, the more value you can see in, and for, yourself. Are you willing to know valuable details about you?

Why do we expect ourselves to know intimate details about others, specifically the person we are dating? Or worse yet, that we must know exactly who we are looking for (the person they are or will be) in order to magically discover (or be discovered by) that special person that we are supposedly destined to meet or the relationship that is "simply meant to be?"

Perhaps it's time to stop looking for "meant to be" and to consider simply being.

So often when we think about desires or goals, we think about what we would like to "get out of life." What I've experienced is that I get the most out of my life when I am not focused on "getting out" of life, but "getting INTO" it. When your intention is to give to you and your life, instead of getting, your receiving will grow abundantly.

Learning to be a giver seems easy, until you realize that you must also be willing to give and receive YOU. That's right, you cannot be a giver until you learn to graciously receive. In order to fully know your value, you must be able to give to you, and open-heartedly receive you...from you.

This includes your likes, dislikes, talents, skills, desires, dreams, imaginations, and creativity. It also includes your attention. When was the last time (or first time) you sat down, paid attention, and listened to you?

Once we meet someone, and begin to get to know them, we start to take an inventory of what they do/may bring to the relationship or our lives. It's time to do the same for you.

We dream of what they are or *could be*! Seriously, ladies…admit it. I am not the only woman who has done this.

A valuable exercise I've done several times in my life is what I call, "My Life Inventory." It's a list of all the resources I have in my life. The people I trust, my support system, anything that I define as valuable. It includes my assets, tangible and intangible, personal and professional. This exercise always helps me feel less alone and less needy, especially after my last divorce. I knew I could count on what I had to not only *"get through,"* but to thrive in the midst of it all and *grow through*.

Every time I take one of my coaching clients through this exercise, profound insights are gained, and her or his conscious value increases exponentially. If you're not aware of your value, it will be difficult to partake in, or share it.

WEEK THREE
THE NO *MEANS KNOW* DATE

Please record your own "Life Inventory" in your *Date Book* this week. No matter where you are in your life, you are where you are. Today is the day to recognize, and *know* where you are, and what/who is in your *now*.

This is also a wonderful time to reach out to the people on your list and thank them for being someone you highly value. Gratitude and appreciation are the most valuable resources you have besides the love in your own heart.

It was the first place I started when I needed a miracle in my life.

> "The more you are grateful,
> the more you will have
> to be grateful for."

When you begin to know and value you, you will discover that saying "No" actually means that you KNOW what's valuable in your life. YOU. It's time to say it, so you can say, "Yes" to your love and life. You are irreplaceable, and so is your time. You are the one who carries your dreams. Say yes to what matters most. Honor the time you're in.

Please invest some special time this week to ask yourself these questions, as well as any others that you have been curious about. Grab your *Date Book* and ask and write until your heart's content.

What is your favorite color? How does it make you feel when you look at it? What word comes to mind to describe this feeling?

What's your favorite number? Why?

Do you have a favorite letter, and if so, why?

What do you do for a living? Are you really living when you are doing it?

How do you spend your time/day?

When do you feel most authentic?

When do you feel most alive?

If you could do anything, and time/money/education were not an issue, what would that be?

If you were a superhero, what would you do? Why? What would you call yourself? Why?

If you could be a supermodel, what would you look like? How would you feel about you?

What is the most beautiful thing you have ever seen?

Do you know how truly irreplaceable you are? How are you irreplaceable?

If you could have the life of your dreams, what would it look like?

How much is your time worth?

What is your hourly rate?

What would you like your hourly rate to be?

Are you willing to exchange your creativity, knowledge, expertise, skills, and/or talents for money instead of exchanging your time for money?

What would that be worth to you each day? Each year?

When was the last time you allowed yourself to dream?

What do you dream about doing? Being? Creating?

I take care of people every day who suffer (or once suffered) from insomnia. In fact, countless numbers of people are plagued with this disturbing condition. It has been my observation, and is my conclusion, that…

> We do not dream due to our inability to sleep, but instead we fail to sleep (or rest) because of our unwillingness to dream.

Energy is abounding in our youth, but so is our skill of playing "make believe," and having grand imaginations. Perhaps energy comes from the practice of play, making, believing, imagining, and dreaming.

Life is quite simply "energy," and if you seem to be lacking in energy it's time to wake up and start dreaming. Your cup or can of a caffeine-ridden energy source isn't going to cut it. Trust me.

Hopefully by now you are getting to know yourself a little more. Not bad after only three dates. Congratulations!

Your fourth date is going to be one that will really take your relationship with you to the next level. On this date you are not only going to be child-like, creative, and fun, but also you will be giving and receiving.

Yes, getting to know you is going to take more than just one or a few dates, so how about another date as soon as possible?

CHAPTER 9

ENGAGEMENT FOUR – *BE YOU*

In order to be fully you, and engaged with your life, it's essential that you take time on a daily (yes, I said *daily*) basis to connect with the true essence of who you are. Often we live our days as a *version* of who we are, but not necessarily the truest version, or the one that is most complete.

We look for others to complete us, which confirms that at the core of this action there is a belief that we are in fact, not whole. Again, this perpetuates the, often unconscious, feeling of not being enough. What is that all about? I've got news for you. It's an epidemic on planet earth! And yes, it affects all of us at least once in our lives. The issue is how long that "once" or "many times" last. For some, it can last a lifetime.

We are not in this world to be completed, but to get a complete understanding of who we are, and are created to be. The more you get to know and understand you, the more you will be able to *be you*...naked and unashamed.

As long as we feel ashamed of who we are, the more we will hide beneath an exterior that is sucking the life out of us. Now, you may be saying to yourself, "Yeah, but I'm not ashamed of who I am." Great! But just to make sure, I want you to answer these questions, "Is there any area of who you are that you reject or ignore? Do you have any aspect of who you are that you do not love? Do you feel as though there is any part of you, your past or personality, that may be unlovable?" If the answer is yes, then I've got some more news for you. And it's good news this time.

Once again allow me to remind you that you're not alone. I have felt this way too. The best part is this: Just because you feel unlovable, doesn't mean you are!

> The only part of you that is unlovable is the part that YOU do not love.

If you had trouble answering any of those questions with a yes, it's a sign that the answer is very likely a no. Also, if your yes was quickly followed by a "but..." then the answer is definitely "yes." What matters most isn't why you feel the way you do, but what matters most is that you acknowledge how, and what you feel. Until you're able to become aware of how you feel, and give *her* loving care and attention regardless of the reason(s), you will block the very thing you desire.

True love doesn't exist in part, and it's not exclusive. It's whole. Genuine love is also very inclusive, and it doesn't require perfection. Love is perfect. It uncovers the imperfections that we bury, and loves them anyway. If perfection were a requirement for love and happiness, none of us would be worthy. It's love that makes us worthy.

When we hold back or ignore an area of ourselves that we feel is dark, imperfect, or unlovable, we hide a part of us that needs to be exposed more than ever. Once it's unburied, the light can shine upon it. Where there is light, there is no dark. Where there is light, there is no heavy. Where there is love, there is light and healing.

Often we live a heavy life because we are carrying unhealthy beliefs that are weighing us down. The guarded misrepresentations, of which we are, as we attempt to hide these feelings of judgment and pain, do not allow our authentic hearts to be expressed or engaged.

Does a tiny bit of dirt on a diamond change the fact that it's a diamond? Or that it was once a piece of coal?

Would you reject a diamond if it had a speck of dust or fingerprints on it? Of course you wouldn't. Imperfections make a diamond unique, and don't change the fact that it's a diamond. Perhaps this may be why it's *a girl's best friend.*

Once you become YOUR best friend, and allow you to be YOU...coal, heat, dirt, dust, fingerprints, imperfections, and all, your capacity to love and be loved exponentially expands.

In order to fully engage, we must first express who we are, fully exposed. Genuinely. Authentically. Once we expose our true selves, then we are able to engage in loving ourselves, and others freely."

"How do I do that?"

Thank you for asking.

By practicing what I call becoming *fearfully fearless.* We all feel afraid at times. Of course we do. So to say that we must always be fearless, is simply not true. But we do have a choice. We can feel fear, and do less. We can feel fear, and do it anyway. Or we can look fear fully in the eyes, fear less, and make it our friend versus our foe.

My little dog used to rarely bark, except when I walked through the door after being away. And she would bark continually until I addressed her. Does fear bark at you? Perhaps all you need to do is acknowledge it, while letting it know that you will not be hanging out with it, but appreciate that it does keep you from doing dangerous things at times.

If you're afraid to let others into a protected place, you may be locking *you* inside of what will soon become your counterfeit, unprotected, prison.

What's the key to getting out and staying out?

Practice the art of being fearfully fearless, and turn F.E.A.R. around. What if we looked at F.E.A.R. another way?

You may have heard two common definitions of fear:

1. "**F**alse **E**vidence **A**ppearing **R**eal" (Thank you, Joyce Meyer)
2. "**F**orget **E**verything **A**nd **R**un" (Thank you, Dr. Jim Richards)

Could you look at it as "truth appearing *not real*?" So the next time what you know to be true looks contrary to your current reality…HAVE NO FEAR. Instead of "Forgetting Everything And Running," let's "remember something and stand!"

> It's time to make a decision.
> You can be afraid of being
> who you are or redefine F.E.A.R.…
> Fully Engage And Remember
> who you are!

When you acknowledge who you are, inside and out, you can authentically and lovingly *be* who you are from the inside out.

WEEK FOUR
THE MAKE ~~OUT~~ IN DATE:

This week it's time to express your creativity. Make a collage that reflects you, your likes, loves, dreams, desires, goals, and imagination. Cut out your pieces and lay them on a background, and when you're finished…take a picture of it. Email the picture to your favorite digital photo finisher, enlarge the picture, print, frame, and voilà...you have a beautiful, one-of-a-kind masterpiece to give yourself. Hang it up, and enjoy!

When your friends and family ask where you got the great piece of art, you can tell them that your date gave it to you. By the way, I would love to see a picture of your final creation.

Once again, I would also like to encourage you to take (or collect pictures) of things that make you feel inspired, creative, and happy. Your life is your collage of what you love, a profound masterpiece!

CHAPTER 10

ENGAGEMENT FIVE – *LOVE YOU!*

Loving you is your greatest ability. This is the heart of the matter, because it's your heart that matters.

Love can be our home. Loving ourselves, and others, is how we live in it... fully engaged.

Several years ago when God asked me if I loved myself, it radically changed the way I see, and experience love. When God asks a question like that, it takes on a whole new meaning. I couldn't speak with words or even think of a response. My life has since become an answer of agreement with the voice of Love.

It was in that moment that the love affair began. The journey continues to this day.

What a beautiful ride it has been!

Now it's time for me to ask you that same question, "Do you love yourself?"

I mean, *really love yourself?*

Hopefully you are beginning to feel the love in a new, and refreshing way. But if you are still having difficulty answering with a resounding, mountaintop proclaiming, "Yes!" it's okay.

What you need is a little more time to spend with you, and get to know you. Gently allowing you time and space to simply be. Acknowledged, nurtured, cared for, appreciated, accepted, and celebrated. Yes, it's possible to build an unconditional love that begins with the courage to *choose* to love you, even if you don't always *feel* like it.

Love is a choice. A decision that we get to make each time we wake up, live from our heart, look in the mirror, walk outside, put food in our mouths, and speak words from it. As well as every moment in between until we lie down at night and breathe a sigh of relief.

Why? Because you remind yourself that, "Today is good because it is. I am also, because I'm loved. And yes, tomorrow is a new day."

YOU bring the love to your life. Love. Life. To bring them together, you must be together and do life together.

There are seven secrets to being in love TO GET HER:

1. **Pursue:** In order TO GET HER, and be a great date, with a great life, you must PURSUE. *Pursuing her* is vital! We need not pursue anyone or anything else. When you pursue your heart, and the ONE that you innately are, you will attract that which you desire. There is no need to pursue that which you can attract.

2. **Priority:** When you become a priority in your own life, you will be a priority. I remember being so heartbroken when my past husband told me I wasn't a priority in his life. It hurt so deeply. Until I realized that the hurt was coming from within me. I was crying to a friend as I told my "Poor Me" story. After I hung up the phone, I heard a wise voice from within ask me if I were a priority in my own life. Honestly, I answered, "No, I am not." The truth was that I had not treated myself as a priority, and I was not a victim. I could (and I did) declare myself a priority in that moment. Ever since then, I have been a priority in my life.

Once I made myself a priority, I passionately allowed my heart to express *herself* fully. I began to see my dreams expressed in new ways, and a new perspective.

3. **Passion:** Passion was no longer simply something I felt inside me, but the "Me" that I passed on to my life and others. Yes, I began to *Pass I On* with no more holding back, slowing down (except to check in with my priorities), or stopping.

   Your passion is not only for you. It's for the world as a whole to see, sense, and savor. When you "pass your I on", your entire life changes, because you express who you are with passion and purpose.

4. **Purpose:** You have a purpose, a very unique one. Did you know this? Do you believe this? Do you know what that purpose is? Whether or not you know it consciously, don't worry. It's there. And when you pursue YOU with passion, your life's priority and purpose will also come out to play, and be romanced. Trust that it's there. Submit to the process of your discovery. Let go, and play.

5. **Play:** It's fun. If you continue to have fun with this process of uncovering, and unveiling, you will be able to take your life off "pause". Turn your life on by playing now, instead of "rewinding" to *a good old day* or attempting to "*fast forward*" to some ideal future. Play your date. Play your day. Play it forward.

6. **Persevere:** I don't think there is any coincidence that the words "sever" and "severe" are in this word, "persevere." In order *to get her* you must be willing to separate out some of the distinct parts of you in order to see them clearly and uniquely. Then by putting them back together again in Holy Union, you will be able to boldly and beautifully reduce the sometimes painful severity of persevering all circumstances in order to be, and stay, together (fully engaged) with your beloved, peaceful self.

7. **Peace:** When you no longer see yourself as missing a "piece" or being a "piece" for someone else, you will begin to experience *peace* like never before. By fully engaging with the experience of becoming whole and fully together within, you will discover that what used to seem hard, and

stressful can be quite easy or as I like to say, "ease-y." Meaning, with an *ease* that defies *dis-ease* or disengagement.

WEEK FIVE
The *I HEART YOU* DATE

Home is where your heart is. This week's date is going to be a beautiful experience of going inside your heart that is your home. After spending much time crying out to God in heartache and suffering, I went on a journey within my heart that transplanted and transformed it.

I saw myself lying on a bed in a well-lit tree house, amidst the trees, in a flourishing rainforest. It was raining light, soothing droplets of life, after the storm had passed. The glowing light from above lit the forest from deep within. The bed on which I lay was covered with a fluffy, down-filled, white comforter. It was behind a flowing mosquito net.

The most sacred women in my life surrounded the bed, and me. My two grandmothers, my mom, and my daughter were there, all dressed in pristine white. The light reflected on their garments, as well as the bedding. There was a magnificent glow surrounding me.

I then saw my heart; the one bleeding in pain, betrayal, ache, and hardship, being lifted out from my chest by a gentle hand. The heaviness of the weight I had carried for so long was no longer present. It was then miraculously replaced with a heart that was filled with love, light, and healing. As quickly as the pain was gone, so was the vision I had just had. However, for hours I continued to feel the glow in my once aching heart. I supernaturally knew my healing had begun, and that I was going to grow again.

After some time had passed, I went on another journey into my heart after spending a morning in prayer and meditation. I saw a long road that led down a small hill. To the right there was a street that led me to a beautiful home on a hill. As I walked up onto the covered porch, and reached out to turn the gold knob on the brilliantly handcrafted red door, I knew that this home was my heart.

I remembered being here years ago, but this time I didn't see what I saw the first time I visited. I don't recall much about the home or my previous visit, except that when I opened the door, I entered into a room that was dimly lit and the walls were bleeding. I never went beyond this room. That was prior to what I now lovingly refer to as my "Heart Transplant."

This visit into my heart was different. I walked into a brightly lit room, but there was nothing else in the house. Where was all the furniture? What happened? Then I heard a still, small voice within me that reminded me that this was my new heart/ home. I was then instructed that I could decorate and design it in whatever way I desired. Wow!

I walked in and saw the vastness of the open space, and the surrounding natural life penetrating the inside, as if they were one. There was no more darkness. It was completely open, and it was my turn to fill it with my creative love and life.

Soon the foyer had a vibrant piece of art on the wall with a light blue background, and yellow, orange, and bright pink flowers welcoming me home. The white marble floor surrounded a small pool in the center of my living room, to the right of the kitchen and to left of the room that would become my bedroom.

Above the pool was a very high, glass ceiling with retractors that allowed not only the sun to pour in, but an opening for gentle rain to land on small streams of lighting that created a fountain-like dance of water, and twinkles above the pool. Between the lighting and the pool was a suspended glass fireplace that allowed the flickers of the fire to be seen from every room in the house.

Straight back was a glass sunroom that became my library of learning, sitting, discovery, prayer and meditation. It has definitely been the most well used place in my home.

I could go on and on. But for now, I will take you on a tour of your heart that is your home. This will not only allow you to discover YOU and what's in you, but to meet some very important people there as well.

Are you ready?

Almost. Please read the following before you begin.

Visualize yourself walking down a long, peaceful, tree-lined road. To the right is a street. You turn the corner and see a home sitting on a small hill on the left. Walk up to the home. What do you notice?

Turn the knob and enter the home. This is your heart.

Walk in, explore, observe what you see and feel. Pay attention. Be. Take whatever time you need to discover each of the rooms and the stories they may share with you.

Whenever you're done exploring, find the most comfortable (or your favorite) room in your home. Sit. Be. Breathe. When you're ready, invite your *little girl*, the younger, smaller, version of you, to come and join you. Spend some time with her. She has a message for you.

Next, invite your older, wiser, peaceful self to join you. How does she look? She will also have a valuable message to share with you.

Once you have spent time with both, please consciously invite the masculine energy within you to come. This is your *little boy* who brings with him the energy that balances that of your *little girl*. Allow him to come and be with you. Notice how you feel in his presence. He has a message for you.

Last, and certainly not least, when you're ready, ask the Keeper of your heart to come. He or she will have a beautiful message to share with you as well.

Once you're ready, open your eyes, and write about all the details of your experience.

Okay. Got it?

Grab your *Date Book* and find a comfortable place where you will be able to experience this special date with no interruptions or distractions. Close your eyes. Take a few deep breaths. Place your hands in your lap with palms up. Relax your head, neck, and shoulders. You're going home.

Have fun!

For years I've spent time in the home that is my heart. Even though my favorite time to do this is in the morning as I start my day, at times it doesn't happen as often as I'd like. Sometimes life gets busy, and I get distracted, and I forget. However, I wonder, "Do I forget because I'm distracted, or am I distracted because I forget?" I believe it's the latter. Nonetheless, when I enter and there is dust on all my furniture, I know it's been too long. However, my little girl, little boy, older, wiser self, and my heart's Keeper (for me this is Jesus) are always there. The conversations we have are always exactly what I need, when I need them. As you can imagine, it has completely revolutionized how I pray. I don't pray, and wait for an answer. Instead, I have a conversation with Love, and we listen.

I suggest that you visit as often as possible, especially when you need to be reminded of the truth. A renewed mind transforms. I believe that a renewed mind is one that is reminded by an open, loving heart. Home is where the heart is, and there is no place like home.

When all is said and done, you don't have to change anything, simply love and be you. That will change everything, including how you *BE*.

Contrary to what many may think, being something, and having an attitude that allows it to be fully expressed can create two entirely different dating scenarios. If you would like to get more than one date, keeping your attitude aligned is everything! Even the greatest individuals can have horribly bad relationships (unhealthy connections or disconnections) because of a bad attitude. Poor attitudes interfere with the full expression of wealth that *is you* (your *WELLTH*).

If you desire to live a life you love, then fully engaging with the attitudes of a great love life are vital. Often we go through life looking for the "engagement". What we miss is the powerful truth that it is WE who BRING the engagement. WE bring the happy, the joy, the energy, the like, the love, the proposal, and the ability to be all these.

The following list of engagements is what I would call, "The Be Attitudes or the Attitudes to Be." It's not a list of how you "should be," but it explains how you already are. When engaging in who you truly are, you can be her, expressing the full life that's in her. This is the key to a great life.

THE PROPOSAL

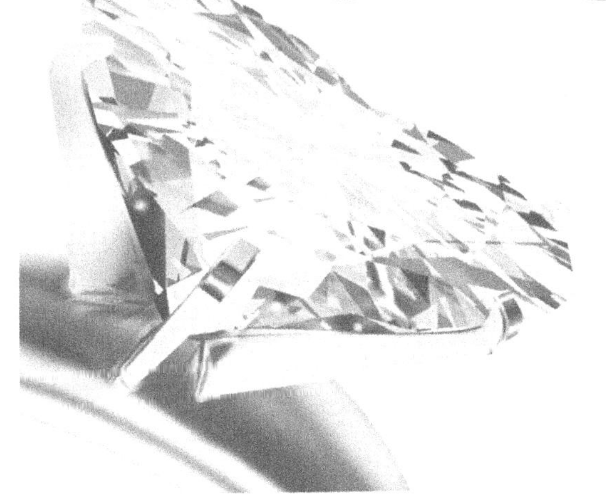

SEVEN
ENGAGEMENTS
OF A
GREAT LIFE

BE LIKE-ABLE
BE DATE-ABLE
BE DREAM-ABLE
BE LOVE-ABLE
BE COMMIT-ABLE
BE ENGAGED
BE MERRY'D

CHAPTER 11

ENGAGEMENT SIX – *BE LIKE-ABLE*

After my first divorce, a well-meaning friend advised me that what I needed to do was to create a list that clearly described my *ideal man*. The advice was founded in her belief that if you truly know what you want, then it's attainable. Since I also had that belief, I enthusiastically sat down and compiled a list. It became a long list of over 100 qualities ranging from "Loves God" to "Loves Seinfeld." I still have that list, and I chuckle when I read it because all of those "requirements" can now be summed up in two simple statements. I must LIKE him. I must trust him.

Likeability has become such a gold standard for me, because frankly my long list really got me into trouble. For some reason it turned a natural, heart-led experience into a cerebral, debatable, inner dialogue that moved me away from being led by my heart, and the indisputable truth that I didn't fully "like" the person I was dating. Yes, I liked a lot of things about him. For example, he had many of the attributes on my "list." But unfortunately, he lacked the most important one: *Being Like-able*. Believe it or not, I actually married him. The "qualified" man by the standards of my infamous list, minus the likeability!

I know that sounds a little hard to believe, doesn't it? Not only a little hard to believe, but not very easy to admit either. It wasn't as though I *disliked* him. But looking back (sometimes a good thing to do momentarily), I realized, "Dang, I never really LIKED him!" It doesn't seem possible to love someone you don't really like, but quite frankly…love seems much more lenient or forgiving than "like" does.

Well, to make a long story short…and a long list very short, I now realize how important LIKE is in a relationship. For me, it was a huge breakthrough, and one that came from the epiphany that what I felt really mattered, and I had a say in the matter. Just because someone measures up on paper doesn't mean that you have to like that person, or God forbid choose to marry him or her! And being likeable is absolutely vital in the relationship that you have with yourself. Yes, you may feel some love towards you, but do you really like you? (The whole you?)

It is very perplexing to me when I think that we as women (or humans) want others to like us, but yet WE do not like us. Hmmm…that is definitely worth pondering, don't you think?

IF YOU DON'T LIKE YOURSELF,
IT'S VERY DIFFICULT TO BE LIKE-ABLE.

WEEK SIX
THE *ME LIKEY* DATE

Create a list of all the things you like about YOU! Then choose a person with which you share a mutual loving, respectful relationship, and read it to them out loud. Invite her/ him to add to it.

NEXT, CREATE YOUR LIST OF "MUSTS" FOR SOMEONE THAT YOU MAY BE INTERESTED IN DATING.

I have included a sample from my previous list (just to name a few) that I hope you find insightful.

- I like him
- I trust him (and the way he sees me)
- I am a priority in his life
- He loves God, himself, and me (in that order)
- He is open-hearted and open-minded
- He is a great friend and chooses friends wisely
- He is honest
- He honors his commitments and his word
- He says what he means and means what he says
- He is kind with himself, me, and others
- He understands himself
- He understands me
- He treats me like a lady—with love and respect
- He says nice things to me/about me (No name calling, ever!) (Hint: Have you ever called yourself fat, ugly, stupid, etc.? Ouch!)
- He loves what he does, and is successful at it
- He is financially independent
- He is a generous giver
- He is humble and asks for help when he needs it
- He listens well and finds out what I like
- He pays attention to how I feel
- He expresses his feelings well
- He asks my opinion and values it
- He celebrates me and likes to plan surprises for me
- He asks me what I imagine and helps it become a reality
- He cherishes me and our relationship
- He takes great care of himself

- He takes great care of those he loves
- He is interested in me and in discovering more about me
- He shares his feelings and compliments freely
- He is observant and listens well
- He spends quality time with me
- He loves to laugh
- He makes me laugh
- He is adventurous
- He plans well for the future
- He lives in the present
- He has a great work ethic
- He is intelligent and wise
- He is very supportive
- He is fun and easy to be around
- He knows me well and seeks to know more
- He loves and appreciates me as I am
- He loves me unconditionally
- He is committed to me and our relationship
- He doesn't compare himself or me to others
- He values family
- He gets along with my family
- He honors my choices
- He is confident and secure
- He is patient
- He is consistent
- He is nurturing
- He is a non-smoker and enjoys exercise (He is healthy!)
- He *Dates Himself Well*

PLEASE DON'T GO ANY FURTHER UNTIL YOU HAVE DONE THIS PART FIRST.

Now, take a look at the list that you just created, and ask yourself, "How am I being that for myself?"

GO THROUGH YOUR LIST AND IDENTIFY THE WAYS THAT YOU CAN BE THESE EXACT THINGS FOR YOURSELF.

If you expect others to love you, treat you well, honor you, respect you, like you, and be a great date...then you MUST be willing to do/be the same for YOU!

This may not be easy for you to hear because perhaps you haven't thought about it in this way. Today is your day. It's time to see things differently; to be the one who loves, dates, and fully engages with YOU.

Be the one who likes you! Be your *Bestie*! Be your best girlfriend!

CHAPTER 12

ENGAGEMENT SEVEN – *BE DATE-ABLE*

In order to be your best girlfriend you must be *date-able*. In my *Pre-Date Myself Well* life, I was definitely more concerned about what I wanted in a date than I was about *being* that date.

What is *date-able?* You and I have already begun this most valuable conversation. Think about the qualities a man would need to have in order to be "dating or marriage" material. What came to mind? Suddenly I can hear a friend of mine defining her lowest standards for dating as she ventured out into the online dating world after her divorce. "Well," she exclaimed, "he should have all of his teeth and a job!" Funny thing is, she actually ended up marrying a wonderful man who did in fact have a job. However, he has no teeth! As it turns out, he was not only date-able, but also an incredible, hard-working man who happens to wear dentures!

Being date-able isn't about whether you have a job, your teeth, or dentures. It's about you being able and available to date. Are you able? Of course you are. Are you willing to make yourself available to YOU? If you are reading this right now, I believe the answer is yes.

Are you willing to enter into a fulfilling life that celebrates the here and now... being fully present to what is? Are you willing to show up?

Often we create a list, and expect another to fit into our rigid requirements. Then we label it as a "relationship," and attempt to fit ourselves into it. Lists and labels won't define love as much as being fully present in it, wearing (metaphorically) what fits, while being stylish and comfortable in the label that is YOU. Being restrained, confined, and pressured about what you "should" be feeling or doing is *not* being date-able.

When I think of "date-able" material, I used to think of "My List". Then, as time went on, my list became much shorter. First I condensed it to "I must respect him. I must trust the way he sees me."

Later it became "I MUST like him...a lot! That means we must understand and 'get' one another. He must have a kind, and loving heart. And of course, I must trust him...a lot."

As my list became more concise, it finally included the "non-negotiables." It also included "I" statements versus "He" statements. Did you notice that?

It really doesn't matter what "he" is or is not. What matters most is what "I" feel and desire. This has way more to do with me, and much less to do with the person that I'm with, although it has a huge impact on the one I choose to date.

Yes, your list of what makes someone "date-able" may include a lot more qualities. However, the more I experience life, I realize that my so-called "LIST" is not nearly as important to me as my number one requirement, and that is: I must remain fully engaged to my heart, remaining true to my first loves: God and Myself. It also keeps me from getting into relationships that don't honor this commitment to my heart.

Are you willing to do this for yourself?

As you contemplate being date-able, it's imperative that you focus on being the greatest girlfriend. You can think of it as being your very own *Bestie*.

Many years ago I did an exercise that helped me get in touch with my *Bestie* (Date-able One). For the first time, I consciously heard her voice, and recognized it as my heart speaking truth to me. In order to do so, however, I needed to first get past the *not so* Date-able One. She is the *Mean Girl*. You can also think of her as the *Bully*. No matter what you decide to name her, know that she is not necessarily your friend, but she is valuable to the relationship you have with you. That is, as long as you don't spend too much of your time dating her.

This exercise allowed the *Mean Girl* to speak her mind (that's where her voice comes from—your mind/head). And girl, did she speak. A lot. You should have heard some of the nasty, mean, degrading, bossy, shaming, blaming, judgmental things she said! I let her speak, as I wrote down and recorded everything she spoke. Finally, she stopped. When she did, I invited my *Bestie* to enter the conversation. It was brilliant. She was soft-spoken, yet articulated with bold, declarative authority. Her words were heartfelt (yep, from the heart), kind, and encouraging. She spoke the truth with love. I felt so happy, comforted, and empowered in her presence. That's why she's my *Bestie*!

Once we were done with the conversation, I thanked them both. I then took all the words that the *Mean Girl* had said, removed them from my journal, rolled them into a ball, and placed them in the fireplace where I lit them on fire. There was no animosity. Instead, there was a high level of awareness and appreciation for the ability to let go of anything that no longer serves me, and the highest form of communication Love.

In a moment of sacred release, I let go.

It's time to meet the date-able, and *not so* date-able, so you can *Be Date-Able*.

WEEK SEVEN
THE *KISS AND TELL* DATE

Are you ready for some great dates with a great girlfriend?

First, grab your trusty *Date Book* and a piece of paper. You guessed it; you're going to have a date with both girls.

Start with a blank piece of paper, so once you're done you can plan a ceremonial celebration of allowing her words to transform into smoke, and rise to the heavens, where they can be replaced with truth. Seriously, this experience can be incredibly profound if you fully engage with both of your dates.

Invite your *Mean Girl* to tell it like it is. Don't worry, she will. You will notice her by the tone that she speaks to you. If she's like my *Mean Girl,* she will usually start off by saying "You... You... You", with an obvious finger pointing and look of accusation. Write down every word on your piece of paper.

When she's done, calmly invite your *Bestie* to share her heart. Wait for her, she *will* speak. Record all her words in your *Date Book*. Give her all the time she needs. Feel her. Hear her. See her. When finished, thank her for being there, always. In ALL ways.

Remember, the *Mean Girl* is not your enemy. She is simply the unloved part of you, thus making her unlovable. You and your *Bestie* have enough love for all three of you. Once you share your love with her, she will not be as mean, nor will she be as scary. Both girls are important, because they represent your head and your heart. Being able to begin to recognize each of their voices will help you determine who you will allow to lead and guide you.

You can also think of your *Mean Girl* or *Bully* as the one who eats from the *Tree of Judgment*. Think of your *Bestie* as the one who eats from the *Tree of Life*. Eat abundantly. Who are you going to spend time with on your dinner date? Where are you going to eat? Which relationship nourishes you most? The choice is yours.

Buy yourself some flowers. Cook your favorite healthy meal, order take-out, or take yourself to your favorite restaurant. Next, slip into some comfortable clothes that make you feel cozy and beautiful. Sit down with a glass of hot herbal tea or wine, and create a list of all the reasons why you're date-able. It's like your own "Personal Ad" that tells everyone (including you) why you are a great date. You've been dating yourself for a while now, so this will be easy (and fun).

Read it aloud in front of the mirror before giving yourself a hug and going to bed. Smile. It's been a great date. Sweet dreams!

CHAPTER 13

ENGAGEMENT EIGHT – *BE DREAM-ABLE*

The most profound thing about the early stages of dating anyone is the element of intrigue. It is filled with possibility and potential. It's an environment that is rich with creative energy, chemistry, and mystery. It lends itself to some of the most compelling dreams and visions of what could be. We hope for the next date, we hope for the future, and we hope for the imaginable "happy ever after."

We dream of being with one another, while often missing the opportunity to be the dreamer, and being in a fully engaged relationship with ourselves.

Are you able to dream? Your "I" will help you.

Consider this.

*What is Relating without the **"I?"***

Without the "I" there is nothing to relate to. Without "I" there is no one to relate with.

So what about the "I?"

***I.** Intrigue inspires interest, and investment. Webster's dictionary defines intrigue as "excite to interest or curiosity." Intrigue is exciting, and where there is excitement* *there is energy and empowerment! When we are intrigued by, or with someone or something, we seek to discover more. It's in this seeking that we also express ourselves.*

What is it that you desire? What are you looking for? What are you expressing? You grow when you're seeking. The finders are the seekers.

In the beginning of all new relationships there is an excitement. Why is that? It's because we are designed to seek. In fact, this is what draws us closer to God, each other, and ourselves. When we're seeking, we are in our most natural form. It's like breathing (or inspiration). It is naturally easy. It doesn't take energy, but gives us energy. We can do it without thinking. It is innate. We invest ourselves, and our time into that which we are interested in. We set out on a path of discovering something new, something we do not yet know. Love begins with discovery...something or someone to love.

There is inspiration in getting to know someone, and sharing that which we know and that which we are, with them. But what happens when we finally know that person, then what? We must celebrate the knowing, and we will have more to celebrate, and more to know.

Where is the intrigue, the excitement? It's in celebrating what we know. When we do, what we know and whom we know will grow. Then there is more to celebrate.

What we celebrate grows! As long as there is growth, there will be life. As long as there is life, there will be growth. And no matter how much we know, there is always something new to discover within ourselves, as well as in others.

Excitement is a magnetic energy in motion that draws people together. This excitement, or intrigue, inspires interest and investment. Excitement is creative. But it can also be created. Investment leads to interest, which inspires intrigue, or excitement.

How do we invest? By sharing who we are, and what we are interested in with those we love, we increase our capacity for love, to love and be loved. This is what it means for us "to give and we shall receive." We share who we are, and who we are grows.

It's a giving, not a taking. It's both sharing, and receiving. We cannot receive if we cannot share. Once a person stops seeking, there is less to share. When we do not share it, there is less to discover and be discovered.

It's not giving if we share it. When we give there is a brief moment that we have "less than" before. But when we share...in that moment (and beyond) both become "greater than." When we share with someone, we both receive. A perfect example is a hug, a kiss, or a touch. The moment we share it, we both receive it. The only thing we are to give is thanks.

This thanksgiving creates celebration (and more opportunities for discovery), which is an atmosphere where what we share grows. Sharing enlarges our capacity to love, for love is not only a feeling. Love is "an ability." Our sharing enlarges this ability (of love) to love and be loved. This ability creates an atmosphere of love, and this is where we live, share and grow...IN love.

The investment of "I" in any relationship is what makes it valuable, interesting, inspiring, intriguing, and eternal. Without "I" there is nothing to relate to. Without "I" there is no one to relate with. The joy is in discovering the "I" who can receive what the "I" has to share.

"I am" equals relationship. It's the relationship of both your heart and head coming together in the revelation that you are here on earth to learn to love...again.

Dream of the "I" that is YOU. Dream of what she likes, loves, and desires. Be all that she is. Allow her to share this intrigue and interest with others in the world. Love the "I Am" that's within you.

Stop holding back. Don't give and take. Share and receive.

Make believe. Make your "I" BE fully present and engaged in the life you live. Dream. Create the life you desire, by creating the love you desire. Don't wait to love. Love now. Love you.

Be the dreamer in your night and day. Shining. No armor, only more of what you dream about. You were created in the image of Love. You are a reflection of that Love.

Give thanks for who you are, and what you love. Begin to share it. Watch what happens as you see through the eyes of a dreamer, living your dreams.

Your dreams are you. Enable them to be awakened. Be YOU, day and night.

WEEK EIGHT
THE *DREAM* DATE

This week's date is going to be one of rest and relaxation. Whether it's a massage, pedicure, or spa treatment, its purpose is to pamper the dreamer.

Then afterward create a heartfelt "DREAM LIST" for your life. Write down 111+ things that you wish you could be, do, or have in your lifetime. Let your imagination go wild. Do not limit yourself by what you think is possible, or hope could happen. Instead, write down everything that you honestly would LOVE to experience in your life. This is a divine opportunity to let your heart lead you. If something comes to mind that seems unexpected, don't self-edit, keep writing and continue dreaming!

Interesting fact: After doing this years ago, I reviewed the list a couple years later and almost ¾ of my list had either happened or was in the process of happening!

Seriously, the only thing more powerful than dreaming is being bold enough to record them…and fully engaged in the process of living them.

CHAPTER 14

ENGAGEMENT NINE – *BE LOVE-ABLE*

The day I became able to love more was the day I tried on a new belief like a new pair of premium denims. You know the ones. They fit, but the more you wear them, the better they feel. And the more *able* you are to love and enjoy them.

My new belief was that I was in fact, *love-able*. After years of dating myself well, and owning my ability to love, I finally released an old belief that had been hidden in my heart far too long. It was the belief that I was not lovable.

I know, it sounds crazy that any human would believe this about her or himself. When in reality, it's not only common, but also a symptom of a much greater cause. Are we feeling unlovable because we are not lovable, or because we have been trying to be something we already are? Thus, creating an epidemic of a whole lot of ~~women and men~~ humans being someone we are not.

We all come to planet earth able to love, being created in the image of Love. Unfortunately, all too often this beautiful truth becomes buried beneath the beliefs of our society, parents, siblings, relatives, friends, circumstances, and soon even ourselves.

One of the first words we're told is "No." Then we're taught to say "No" to our dreams and imaginations, by saying "Yes" to everyone, and everything else. While saying "No" to our passions, dreams, and loves seems to be the norm, it doesn't make it "the truth." But it can become *your truth*, until you're brave enough to believe *the truth* about you, love, and life. The truth is that you are *love-able*, which automatically makes you lovable.

Your ability to love is possible, because love IS limitless possibility.

Have you ever noticed that "possibility" contains three "I"s? Possibility becomes reality when we are willing to allow our eyes to see the "I" differently. Are you willing to believe something new about you? Are you open to believing that you already possess that which you seek? Can you define love differently then you have in the past?

What would your life look like if you defined love as patient, kind, free of jealousy, not boastful, without pride, honoring, not seeking itself, non-judgmental, delighting only in good, rejoicing with truth, and always protecting, trusting, hoping, and persevering?

What if love never fails?

Would this mean that when you love yourself deep in your soul, because you are *love-able*, you succeed?

Imagine if you could love like this? Live like this?

This is the infinite possibility of love, true love.

So let's talk about this thing called love. Remember, the opposite of love is not hate, but fear. Are you brave enough to open yourself, and your heart, to the possibility of loving yourself in a whole new way? To love you the way God loves you? Unconditionally.

What if you truly are a masterpiece?

What if you could accept YOU as a beautiful, creative gift?

It's time to give thanks, my dear, for the love in you, the love that is you, and most of all, the Love that made you.

Often we view ourselves with so much judgment, causing unnecessary suffering and shame. What if you had the power to join YOUR team once and for all? By working for you, and not against you, it allows you to *sip on life* in a way that satisfies the thirst of the soul.

The next time you feel compelled to judge you, or someone else, choose appreciation as an alternative. Often it's our differences that allow us to love our similarities more. Love is that similarity.

Learn to recognize moments of wonder, moments of marvel. These are opportunities to love. Loving yourself in this way is highly attractive. You don't have to pursue that which you can attract. If you desire more love in your life, love more.

How do you show love? How do others show love to you? Do you know your love language? One of my favorite books is, "The Five Love Languages" by Gary D. Chapman. In it he talks about the five primary languages of love. I highly recommend you read the book or check out his website to help you discover your primary love language. That way, you will best know how to show yourself (and others) love. It truly is a lovely thing.

I often wonder if the commandment to love others as we love ourselves has been a fundamental stumbling block. Hmm? It's wonderful if we, in fact, love ourselves. Yes, if people truly loved themselves, then there would be no such thing as war. It would be all peace and love! But contrary to that beautiful ideal, most people do not, and therefore we make war and not enough true love.

It is in loving ourselves well, that we are able to love others well.

We have all heard about the Golden Rule. To treat others as we would like to be treated seems like a good habit to practice. However, we mustn't forget to include ourselves in that list of "others." To help you, I have created a new Golden Rule (with a twist or "shine"). I call it the "Diamond Rule."

> The Diamond Rule is,
> "People will treat you
> the way you treat you."

So often we do so much for others, and neglect ourselves, while unconsciously thinking that eventually "they" will do the same for us. And finally our needs will be met. I have personally discovered how dangerous this can be. If we are not willing to acknowledge our needs, and care for ourselves, why would anyone else?

It is only when we are cared for that we can care for others well. And it is when we have learned and practiced the art of dating ourselves well, that we can perhaps do the same with others.

WEEK NINE
THE *TALK LOVEY TO ME* DATE

This week I would like you to go to discover your primary love language. Please go to: www.5lovelanguages.com and take the Five Love Languages test. I have no affiliation with this company or site, nor do I receive anything for recommending it. I do, however, recommend it to my clients and appreciate the perspective it can offer when thinking of *dating yourself well,* and being in relationship with others. Depending on your primary love language, your date this week will be one* of the following:

QUALITY TIME: If you are a quality time girl then plan a date that creates and savors quality time with you.

ACTS OF SERVICE: Are acts of service your language? Then plan a date where you do something for you...perhaps it's cleaning out and organizing your closet, getting your vehicle detailed, or whatever "it" that's been on your "should do" list and would make your life easier.

PHYSICAL TOUCH: Perhaps you are someone who experiences love through physical touch. Then it's time to plan a date that includes a massage or a facial.

WORDS OF AFFIRMATION: If words of affirmation are your big hit, then plan a date that includes writing a list of loving, encouraging words that you can read daily, but also out loud...IN FRONT OF THE MIRROR! Are you feeling the love yet?

RECEIVING GIFTS: Gifts may be the way you receive love. If so, plan a date that involves you buying (or making), and giving yourself something that makes you feel extra special.

*You don't have to limit yourself to only one date this week. Feel free to try more than one, or all of them. A girl can never have too much love or too many dates. Although, you will likely find that you enjoy one or two more than others.

CHAPTER 15

ENGAGEMENT TEN – *BE COMMIT-ABLE*

Recently I read an article that was instructing people on how to be a great girlfriend or boyfriend, and top on the list was "Keeping Your Word." Everybody wants to date someone who says what they mean, and means what they say. Not as many are willing to be that person.

It's become acceptable to commit to something, and not follow-through. Divorce rates are proof of it. But what about the smaller commitments, like showing up where and when you say you will?

We say one thing, and too often do another. Someone once told me that the definition of integrity is honoring your word. He said that, "I am my word." I've never thought about integrity or commitment quite the same way since then. It's definitely a new standard.

Or perhaps you remember every promise you make, you show up every time, and on time, but what about the rest of us? I believe we, including myself, could improve in this area.

But yet, we are all guilty of breaking promises to ourselves constantly.

If we didn't, the workout gyms would be as packed on July 1st as they are on January 1st. Unfortunately we don't honor our resolutions, commitments, or promises.

The number one excuse for most people is not having enough time. As we've already discussed, that's simply a misconception.

When you love the time you're in, it can love you back. But what happens if it doesn't? Is there a cure?

I'm not sure if it's a cure, but because I believe in finding the cause versus simply looking for a symptomatic cure, let's get to the heart of the matter.

There is definitely hope.

As you have heard me say many times, hope is everything! It's foundational to healthy, happy living. Why? It's because hope is more than a positive expectation.

Hope is also belief, desire, and trust.

Our beliefs direct our actions. Enough said. If you continue to act, or not act, a certain way, it's not behavior modification that's needed. Instead, it's releasing an old, limiting belief that makes way for a new one. Often, we are highly motivated to start something new, but not inspired enough to follow-through and finish what we started.

The list of "To-Do's" increase, while our "To-Done's" wane.

> Master multi-taskers must also become master multi-finishers.

If what you desire is not congruent with your beliefs, chances are, it's simply not going to happen. Either your beliefs must change, or your desires. If they are not united and fully engaged with one another, neither will you!

Your desires will only go as far as your beliefs will allow. In order to be "Commit-able", you must be "Believe-able." And in order to be believable, one must be trustworthy.

Often we question our desires, and wonder if we can achieve them. When the answer to our question is determined by whether or not our beliefs are worthy of our trust. If they are not, then it's time to get a new belief(s). You and your desires must be able to trust your beliefs in order for YOU to commit to your desires.

This is what it means to be *Believe-able.*

Being *Commit-able* means, being *Believe-able, Desire-able,* and *Trust-able.*

Commitment is also synonymous with engagement. When you are fully engaged with your desires and beliefs, you are also not only able to commit, but you (and others) can trust you as well.

Are you trustworthy with your time? Is the "I'M" in your T(I'M)E ready to commit to engaging with it, and being worthy of *your* trust?

It's a great date to start.

WEEK TEN
THE *PINKY PROMISE* DATE

For your date this week, please commit to a day or night that you will prepare for like you're going to one of the most important meetings ever. Set the time and place. Shower, dress in your favorite outfit, and present yourself like you mean business. After all, this is your life that you're going to be talking about. Show up prepared to account for how you have been spending your time for the past year. Bring your schedule, and your *Date Book.* After reviewing your calendar for the past year, ask yourself if this is how you would love to be spending your time. Then, tell yourself what you would rather be doing. Record every delicious detail in your *Date Book.*

How do you desire to spend your day? Not so much as what you want to *do,* but how you would like to *live*? How do you desire to spend your day(s)? How would you like to *date your day*?

Don't hold back. This is the time to *commit* to your day.

Watch and see. Instead of your schedule or calendar being your life, your *Date Book* can become your new "datebook" and way of living.

It's time to Save the Date. Your Date!

CHAPTER 16

ENGAGEMENT ELEVEN – *BE ENGAGED*

Now that you've defined your *ABLE-ity*, all that's left is full engagement with, and in, your abilities.

Your ability to meet you is being brave enough to see you for who you are now. Not who you once were. When you perceive yourself from the perspective of presence, you become aware of all that you are up to this point. In fact, I'm going to let you in on a little, yet hugely profound secret: YOU are not your past or your future. The only place that you can be present is in the present. The best news about that is you don't even have to concern yourself with releasing yourself from your past. You were never *IT* to begin with!

If you concern yourself with it, you will tend to look at your life as the sum of many parts. Instead, you are the only LIFE that's in your life. You are not a total sum of the pieces in your life. You are the whole piece, and you are the carrier of peace.

Often we think of our lives as a series of events that happen to us, or those that we create. When in essence, we are the *life* that comes to the existence of what is, and we define how we are going to see, and live it. Living it is simply how we choose to interact with the life that we *are,* and creating the experience of it that we *desire.* Again, you are not the past or the future. You are life in the present.

Engage with YOU here, now, in this moment. Be you. As you look to the future, prepare yourself to bring something remarkably creative and valuable to it. YOU!

Recently I heard the greatest definition of life. It came out of the mouth of a fifteen-year-old young man who said that life is love. He then went on to say that God is love. Yes, love is the most excellent of all. I couldn't agree more.

> Is life what's happening to us,
> or the ability to create
> with the love that's in us?

You're fully able. Are you willing?

Be present, fully present—that is the gift of full engagement.

Be engaged and engaging…this will empower you to be the great lover of your life.

WEEK ELEVEN
THE *PUT A RING ON IT* DATE

It's time to go shopping for a tangible symbol of you and your abilities, and full engagement with them. To you!

That's right, I'm talking about ring shopping. Take your time finding the perfect ring for you. Whether it's a right-handed diamond, cubic zirconia, or whatever makes you smile. The key is that you love the ring. You will wear it as a reminder of your commitment to love yourself and be fully engaged, beyond "until death do you part."

If you are not a ring wearer, then select a piece of jewelry that best suits you. It's your engagement, and there are no rules. Well, that is except being fully engaged with yourself, your life, and engaged in all you are, and all that you do. Otherwise your ring will only be a symbol of another broken promise.

If jewelry is simply not your thing, perhaps it's a new pair of the most incredible shoes. They will be a reminder of the shoes (your shoes) that you've walked in, along with the many steps that brought you to this day. You could also choose a fabulous handbag or perfect new luggage that will accompany you to places you have never been. Allowing this new baggage to remind you that you have released your old baggage, and it's time for a new journey.

Before you give yourself this "Engagement Gift," plan a special date where you will once again meet with you and your trusted *Date Book*. Please answer the questions: What does being fully engaged *to me*, and *in my life*, mean to me? What does it look and feel like? How would I like to wear this new engagement? I am committing to: ________(fill in the blank)________.

Once you have written what's on your heart, and purchased the right engagement gift for you, please stand in front of your mirror, and read your answers out loud to yourself. Make a promise to commit to what you've shared. Hey, you may even get down on one knee.

Sign your commitment, giving yourself permission to be fully engaged to *the great lover of your life*. Remember, a great lover keeps her word. A great lover honors her commitments, especially those she makes with herself. Give yourself the gift as a tangible reminder of your engagement. Most of all, giving yourself the invaluable present of being fully engaged with YOU in it.

YAY!! Now give yourself a hug, please!

Congratulations! I'm so proud of you!!

Now it's time to be "Merry'd" and share your engagement with your life, and those in it.

CHAPTER 17

ENGAGEMENT TWELVE – *BE MERRY'D*

And the YOU shall become ONE.

Yes, it's your Big Day. It's a public declaration of UNITY. The unity of your head and heart, your heart and soul, your happy and healthy, your little girl and you, your little girl and boy, your *happy* and *ever after*. It's YOU being MERRY, and not waiting for Christmas to do it, but declaring your love boldly and beautifully on this, your very special day.

You can get gifts, but unless you receive them, they are not yours. Today is your day to receive the gift of all that you are, and will be, as you fully engage with you, and share you with yourself and others that you love.

This week you will take your engagement to a whole new level of commitment. Declare your love for being merry, and bringing the merry to your life.

It's your date to plan and pursue it.

WEEK TWELVE
THE *BE MERRY'D* DATE

Plan and have a party with your closest family and friends in attendance. Gifts required: Gifts that honor you and your special day. Everyone wears your favorite color, and you wear a special outfit, your new jewelry (or pair of shoes), with your bags packed and ready to go on this new journey called "Your Fully Engaged Life."

Once you've had your *Ceremonial Celebration,* plan to take yourself somewhere. Perhaps somewhere you've never been.

You are going to take yourself on an excursion. It can be something simple like your favorite coffee shop or a picnic in the park. You can also plan something much more elaborate, like an overnight (or several nights) trip out of town.

As I said, it can be as simple or elaborate as you desire it to be. The only requirement is that you choose to do whatever your heart feels happy doing. If you plan to do something that will take time to plan, put your whole heart into it. Start planning today. No matter what, do something today with your heart leading you. Because this is your day, and you can rejoice and be glad in it.

Do not allow time, space, finances, anyone, or anything, to limit your choices. If you can (I'M)agine it, your I AM can create it.

If you choose to take someone with you, that's totally fine. There are no rules! This is your celebration of *Being Merry'd.*

Of course, you're always welcome to join me, and other lovely women like yourself, at a *LIVE Date Yourself Well C.A.M.P.*

Please allow me to be the first to congratulate you on your commitment and engagement to *Being Merry'd.* I celebrate you in being the great lover of your life!

P.S. THE *HAPPILY EVER AFTER* – BE(YOU)TEA-FULL S.O.L. DATES

BE your beautiful self. BE full as you *Sip On Life*. BE fully engaged. BE the great lover of your life. Attract that which you desire. Do not pursue that which you can attract. Grab a delicious cup of your favorite tea, your *Date Book*, and favorite pen. I've added some extra pages in the back of the book for this very special *S.O.L. DATE*.

What's your story? Begin to write your very own unique *S.O.L. STORY* on the following pages. Include where you've been, lessons learned, where you are, *who* you are, where you desire to be, what you believe, who/what you trust, and *YOUR ULTIMATE TRUTHS*. This is your new love story.

My journey began in South Africa, and has included many *S.O.L. DATES* since then. In fact, I began to meet with a very wise and dear couple that was (and still are) instrumental in my journey.

For years we met almost every week to share and discuss life as we know and live it in the moment. What began as a safe place to go, and speak about my painful feelings and emotions, evolved into a much larger space of soulfully being present and aware.

This transition happened the instant I made the decision to stop talking about my problems and pain, and instead, become fully present to all possibilities. My mentors were more than happy to hear this."Imagine what life would be like if we became open to seeing what it provides, while fully embracing and engaging with it?" This is what we asked ourselves, as well as of each other.

They told me that for years they had desired to meet with like-minded people to contemplate and converse about the beauty of life, and the possibilities in and of it. Instead, working many years as counselors, they met with countless numbers who were so busy suffering, and looking for solutions, they never fully engaged in the process of allowing her or himself to be the *SOLution.*

The moment I engaged with being my *SOLution,* my life completely transformed. So can yours.

I used to joke at our weekly meetings and say, "Some people get together to drink, eat, gossip, etc. We get together to ***S**ip **O**n **L**ife.*" Being the acronym lover that I am, our meetings instantly became our *S.O.L. DATES.*

These are the rules for our *S.O.L. DATES* and the New Rules *(Agreements)* for *S.O.L. Dating* Yourself Well:

S.O.L. DATE AGREEMENTS

1. Show up (Meet You)
2. Only pay attention to what has heart and meaning (Know You)
3. Don't use blame, guilt, or judgment with anyone, including yourself (Value You)
4. Be open to outcome, but not attached to it (Be You + Love You!)
5. If something can't be interpreted two ways, it probably isn't true.
6. You're always telling your story; Are you listening?

WHAT'S YOUR STORY? I WOULD LOVE TO LISTEN.

Please join our special *Date Yourself Well* Facebook Page for weekly *S.O.L. DATES* at www.facebook.com/dateyourselfwell (You can think of it as your very own S.O.L. Support.) I/We would love to hear from you, about your journey, your *S.O.L. DATES*, and anything else you would like to share that will help all of us Date Ourselves Well.

THE ULTIMATE BE. BEgin...

Be a priority and love yourself unconditionally with more Certainty + Abundance + Movement + Purpose.

BE YOUR HAPPILY EVER AFTER...

Thank you for allowing me the incredible opportunity of sharing this time with you over the past twelve weeks (and longer). It has been my absolute pleasure to speak to your heart, and share mine with yours. Thank you in advance for helping me to share this with as many hearts as possible. I love and appreciate you!

The journey continues...remember, it all starts with a date. ☺

Your *S.O.L.* Sister

xo

Dr. Shannon

IT ALL STARTS WITH A DATE!

Keep track of your favorite dates so you can repeat them in the future, although I would encourage you to continue to come up with new, fresh ideas to romance your heart and soul. Also, if you ever get asked about your favorite things to do on a date, you can pull out your list.

1. THE *NAKED AND UNASHAMED* DATE
2. THE *GETTING DOWN (AND NOT SO DIRTY)* DATE
3. THE *NO MEANS KNOW* DATE
4. THE *MAKE ~~OUT~~ IN* DATE
5. THE *I HEART YOU* DATE
6. THE *ME LIKEY* DATE
7. THE *KISS AND TELL* DATE
8. THE *DREAM DATE*
9. THE *TALK LOVEY TO ME* DATE
10. THE *PINKY PROMISE* DATE
11. THE *PUT A RING ON IT* DATE
12. THE *BE MERRY'D* DATE

P.S. THE *HAPPILY EVER AFTER...*(S.O.L. DATES)

MEET THE AUTHOR

Shannon "Dr. Shannon" Gulbranson, B.S., D.C.

coach | speaker | author | entrepreneur | chiropractor

Dr. Shannon is the Founder and C.E.O. (Caring Empowered Owner) of *Healing Life Coaching, Inc.* and *Date Yourself Well C.A.M.P.* Her Minneapolis + New York City based consulting company provides Life Coaching to individuals and corporations throughout the United States, Canada, and Australia. She is also an inspiring international speaker and best-selling author.

Serving thousands of patients for over two decades in private practice, as well as one of the leading cancer hospitals in the world, she has become an expert in engaging the head + heart and healing the heart + soul. She uses her experience as a healthcare and fitness professional, life coach, and entrepreneur to help individuals discover their *WELLTH,* and become fully engaged with who they are and the life they desire.

Dr. Shannon is on a mission to partner with those who desire MORE to become clear, fully engaged, and in love with their life + life's work so they can express Hope + Energy + Awareness + Love, doing what they love and inspiring others to do the same.

Her greatest honors are that of being mom to her beautiful daughter, a *Messenger of Hope* to those in need of healing, and empowering women of all ages to *Date Themselves Well.*

To meet Dr. Shannon and receive free resources, send pictures or comments about your journey, or to schedule Dr. Shannon to speak, please contact:

Dr. Shannon
Healing Life Coaching, Inc.
www.doctorshannon.com
www.doctorshannonblog.com
www.facebook.com/dateyourselfwell

MY S.O.L. STORY

(It's time to write your personal love story.)

MY
S.O.L.
STORY

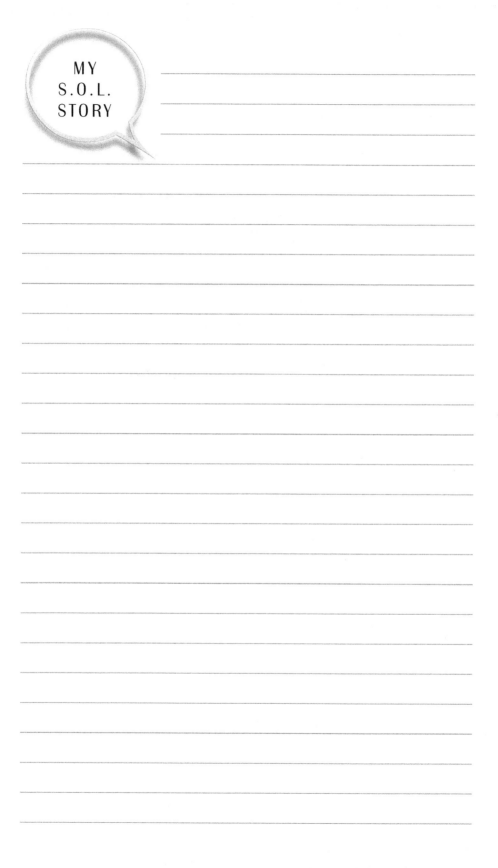

MY
S.O.L.
STORY

MY
S.O.L.
STORY

MY
S.O.L.
STORY

MY
S.O.L.
STORY

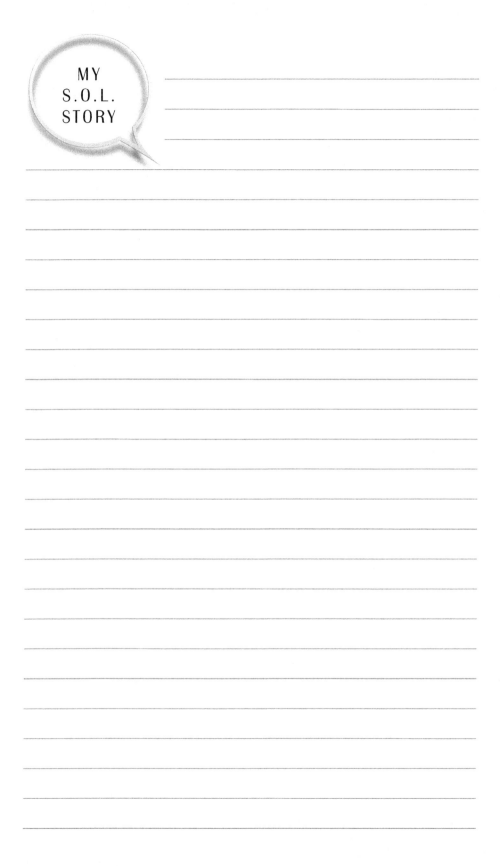

MY
S.O.L.
STORY

MY
S.O.L.
STORY

MY
S.O.L.
STORY

MY
S.O.L.
STORY

MY
S.O.L.
STORY

MY
S.O.L.
STORY

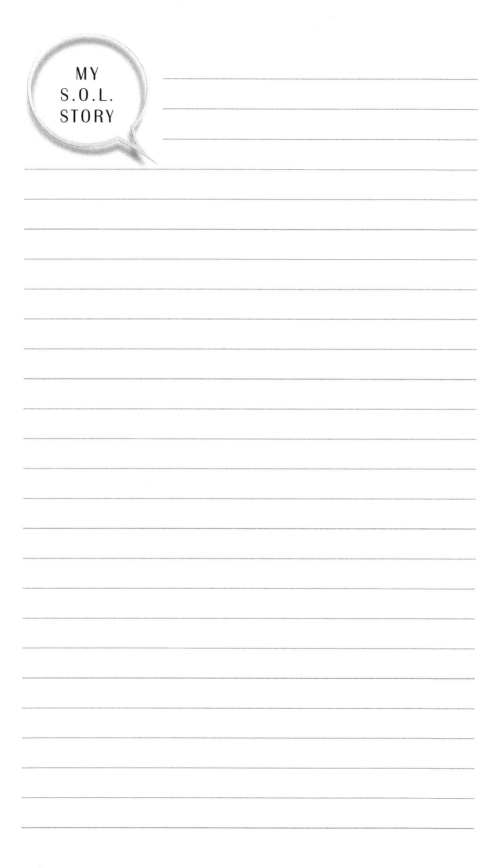

MY
S.O.L.
STORY

MY
S.O.L.
STORY

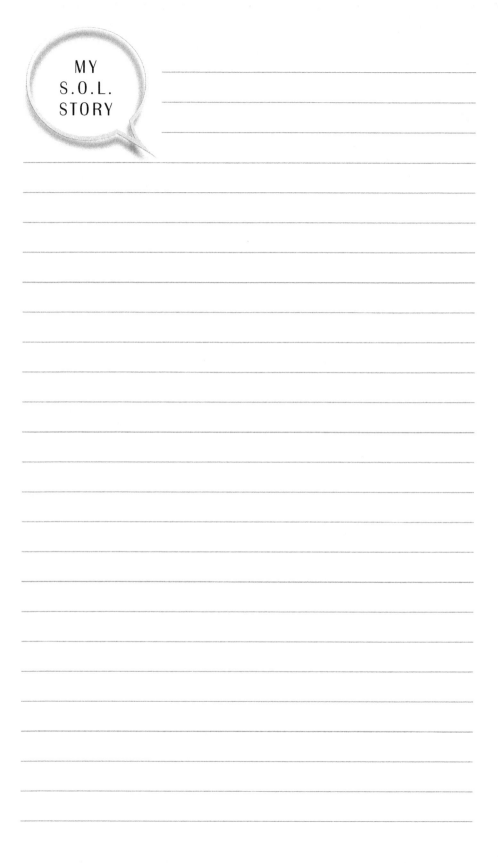

MY
S.O.L.
STORY

MY
S.O.L.
STORY

MY
S.O.L.
STORY

MY
S.O.L.
STORY

MY
S.O.L.
STORY

MY
S.O.L.
STORY

MY
S.O.L.
STORY

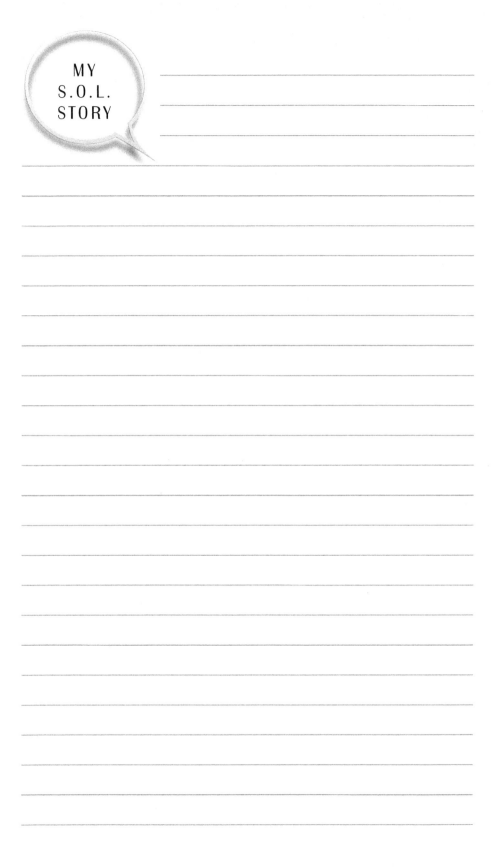
MY
S.O.L.
STORY

MY
S.O.L.
STORY

MY
S.O.L.
STORY

MY
S.O.L.
STORY

MY
S.O.L.
STORY

MY
S.O.L.
STORY

MY
S.O.L.
STORY

MY
S.O.L.
STORY

MY
S.O.L.
STORY

MY
S.O.L.
STORY

MY
S.O.L.
STORY

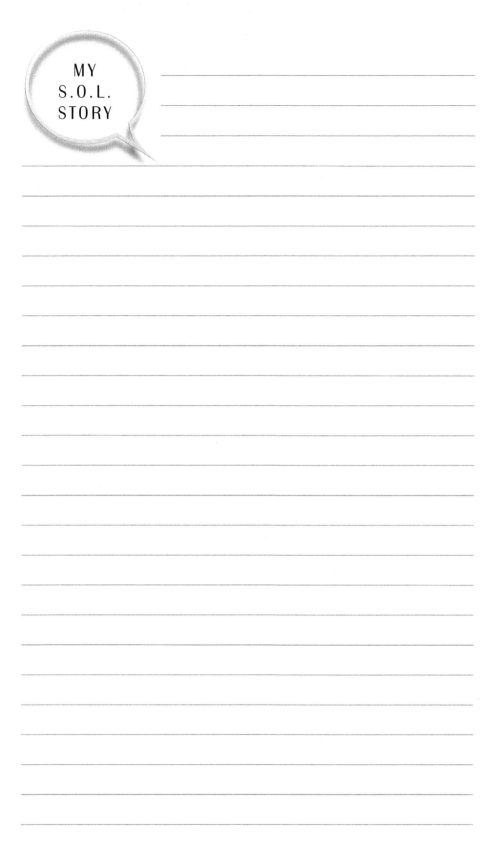

MY
S.O.L.
STORY

MY
S.O.L.
STORY

MY
S.O.L.
STORY

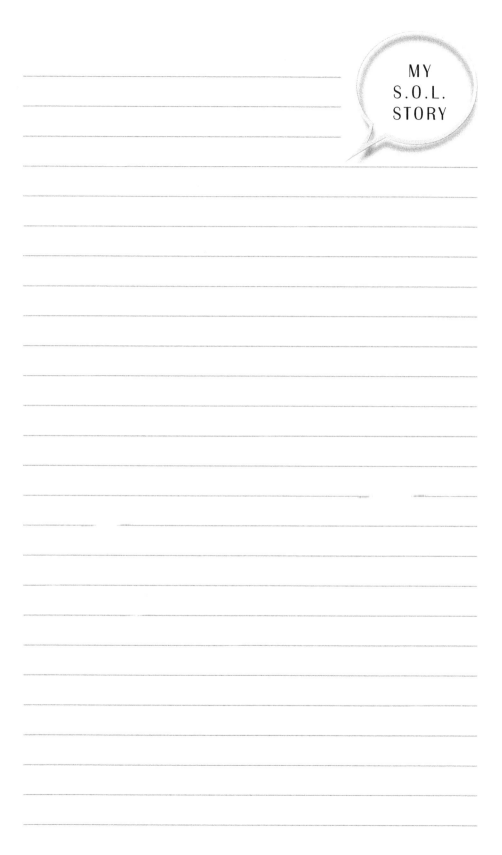

MY
S.O.L.
STORY

MY
S.O.L.
STORY

MY
S.O.L.
STORY

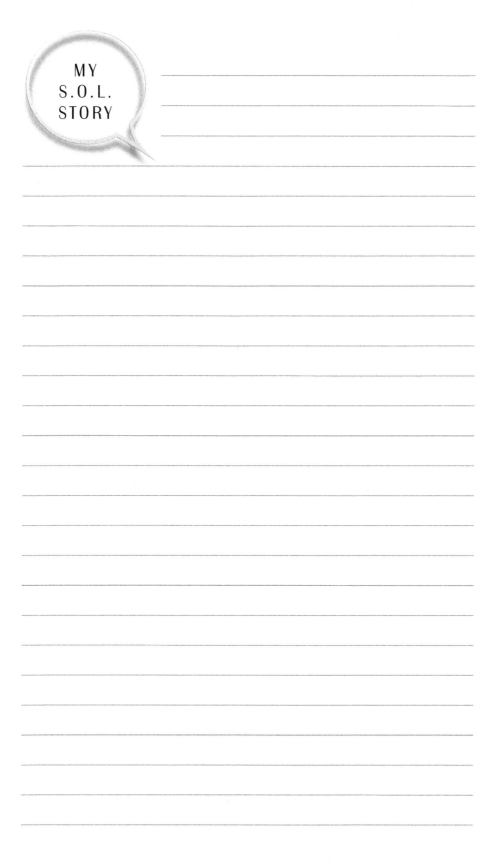

MY
S.O.L.
STORY

MY
S.O.L.
STORY

MY
S.O.L.
STORY

MY
S.O.L.
STORY

MY
S.O.L.
STORY

MY
S.O.L.
STORY

MY
S.O.L.
STORY

MY
S.O.L.
STORY

90132897R00098

Made in the USA
Columbia, SC
27 February 2018